HAUNTED OHIO IV:

Restless Spirits

CHRIS WOODYARD

Kestrel
Publications

1811 Stonewood Drive
Beavercreek, OH 45432

ALSO BY CHRIS WOODYARD

Haunted Ohio: Ghostly Tales from the Buckeye State
Haunted Ohio II: More Ghostly Tales from the Buckeye State
Haunted Ohio III: Still More Ghostly Tales from the Buckeye State
Spooky Ohio: 13 Traditional Tales
The Wright Stuff: A Guide to Life in the Dayton Area
Spooky America: 30 Traditional Tales (in progress)

First Edition 1997
Printed in the United States of America by C.J. Krehbiel, Cincinnati,
OH
Typesetting by Copy Plus, Dayton, OH
Cover Art by Larry Hensel, Hensel Graphics, Xenia, OH
Library of Congress Catalog Card Number: 91-75343

Woodyard, Chris
Haunted Ohio IV: Restless Spirits / Chris Woodyard
SUMMARY: Tales of ghosts and haunted houses from around Ohio.

ISBN: 0-9628472-5-9
1. Ghosts
2. Ghost Stories
3. Ghosts—United States—Ohio
4. Ghosts—Ohio
5. Haunted Houses—United States—Ohio
6. Haunted Houses—Ohio
I. Woodyard, Chris II. Title
398.25 W912H
070.593 Wo
Z1033.L73

To Jan and Louise, who keep Kestrel flying

and

To Marsha, who saved the day

ACKNOWLEDGMENTS

Anonymous (including the lady who introduced me to her mother who told the polar bear skull story—your name must have been written in invisible ink on my notes.), David A. Baer, Kaalem Bailey, Sheila Kneff Ballinger, Angela Ballow, Ed & Cindy Barmick & the gang, Nora Basinger, Devin Bennett, Sue Benton, Teresa Beres, Cheryl Blazek, Krista Botjer, Jeanne E. Burlile, Valryn Bush, Connie Cartmell, Art Caruso, Cathy Christian, Charles Clark, Richard L. Cooley, Mark Cory, Josh Couts, Brian W. Cordial, Dorothy Cox, Elaine Crane, Karen Crawford, Richard Crawford, Anne Cruse, Rob & Kathy Cyphers, Jerry & Mary Day, Candi Dillon, Ruth & William Dixon, Dan Flinchum, Mike Garrett, Jeremy Geahlen, Angela Granata, April Grigsby, Chris Groaner-Fink, Alan Hall, Pub. Lib. of Steubenville, Mike Hall, Marsha Hamilton, Martha Hardcastle-Guthrie, Thomas E. Havelka, Shanon Hazel, James S. Henry, Alison B. Hernan, Andrea Hervey, Ursula Hertenstein, Wallace Higgins, Bruce Hill, Rebecca Hoelle, Julia Holland, Dutch & Lynn Holmer, Lynn Howard, Officer Jones, Ruth Marie Keffer, Steven & Judy King, Kevin Kincer, Glenn & Patricia Kittles, Jan Kleinhenz, Kiersten Knore, Freeda Kohl, Walt Kumbusky, Bob Ladd, Elizabeth Langguth, C.S. Lathrop, Auglaize County Historical Society, Ed Leen, Jane Leen, Gayle K. Lewis, Mindy Liechty, Matt & Vicki Loveday, Gilda Lynch, The Majestic Theatre; Carol Machinga, Ken & Sue Magnuson, Linda Marcas, Frances E. McCoy, Jim McGuire, Sigie Mingie, Joy Moore, Lois Neff, Ashley Noffsinger, Vivian Noggle, James C. Oda, Piqua History Coordinator, Louise Olson, Anne Oscard, Marti Oyer, Lisa Perry, Mary Preston, Dave Reese, Tom Robinson, Janet Rogers, Karen Romick, Ross Co. Hist. Soc., Jim Sands, Toni Seiler, Darke Co. Hist. Soc., Rod Senter Jr., Dave "Casper" Shahan, Kim Shepherd, Dave Shulaw, Donna Simmons-Maier, Neil & Willa Jean Smalley, John Smith, Melissa Smith, Louise E. Stange-Wahl, Michael Stutz, John Switzer, L. Gregory Thurston, Chris Tuell, Elaine Vanderschrier, Vern Oakley, Marlene Waechter, Don Walker, Cincinnati Heritage Tours; Charles B. Wallace, Harrison Hist. Soc., Jessica Wiesel, Dave Westrick, Bill Wild, David Winter, Nanette Young, Roz Young, Barbara Zahniser and the Reference Staff at the Beavercreek Library.

A special thanks to my researcher Curt Dalton, who deserves a medal for some of the quests I sent him on.

If you see your name here and have moved in the last six months, please call me at 1-800-31-GHOST so I can make sure you get your free copy. I apologize if I have accidentally left anyone out.

TABLE OF CONTENTS

Introduction

Prelude: Dead Man Walking

INTRODUCTION

*If I saw it, it might be a ghost and it would scare
me badly because I don't believe in ghosts.*
-John Steinbeck-

Why should there not be ghosts?
-Carl Jung-

Do you believe in ghosts?

Whenever I'm asked that question I reply, "I absolutely,
positively, don't know." I'm acutely aware that I can't prove
one syllable of any of these stories. Ghosts won't perform on
cue before the cameras. They can't be caged in a lab and made
to do their tricks. The "evidence" I offer is purely circumstan-
tial. It does add up, but ghosts still remain tantalizingly elusive
creatures.

Sincere people tell me plausible stories about strange
experiences. I believe *they* believe something supernatural
happened to them. I've seen things myself that shouldn't be
there, but then, I could just be insane or mistaken or making
this all up, couldn't I?

But when I go into a house I know nothing about and see
the same exact things in the same exact places as the owners
have experienced, what does that mean? Am I reading their
minds? I simply don't know. A lifetime may be too short to
find out.

At a school appearance, after hearing how much ghosts
scare me, one child asked me, "Why don't you stop?"

The question stopped me cold. Why don't I? Why do I go
in search of forces that leave me drained and exhausted? Why
do I seek out the very things that terrify me?

For one thing, it is both appalling *and* exhilarating at the
same time. For another, I always want to know—was this time
just a fluke? Can I do this again? And, I suppose it's much like
mountain-climbing: because it's there—or perhaps *not* there...

In ghosthunting these days I find that I usually only have to distinguish between two kinds of ghosts: the "memory ghosts" and the "conscious" ghosts. Memory ghosts are "recordings" of strong emotions or traumatic events. They are simply images with no consciousness, no will, no direction. They replay events from the past over and over, almost like a tape loop.

A conscious ghost seems to be aware of itself and others. They appear to be able to see me; sometimes they try to communicate; they seem to still have their personalities more or less intact. And they can still *want*, which is sometimes the most terrifying thing of all.

But do these ghosts actually exist? Or are they just symptoms of our modern anxiety, creations of a disordered mind, or merely bad dreams brought on by too many nachos before bedtime?

I always answer: absolutely, positively I don't know.

But do *you* believe in ghosts?

Come away with me now, on a tour of Ohio's haunt-spots, where, as you will see, the spirits are restless. Then, make up your mind.

NOTE: Names with one asterisk mean that the name was changed (1) by request of the person involved or (2) because I couldn't find the person and ask permission to use their real name. If you are one of these persons and are surprised to see your story here, please contact me.

DEAD MAN WALKING

Dead men drag earthward
-J.R. Tolkien-

I can't get away from ghosts, even on my vacations. That first night at the Ft. Magruder Inn in Williamsburg, Virginia, I woke up with the feeling you get when someone is standing behind you. Uneasily, I rolled over, only to be confronted by a ghastly sight: a young Civil War soldier standing by the bed, staring at me. He was very young—no more than 15 or 16— and wore light-colored, brownish-grey clothing. Half of his face had been shot away. I had never before seen a headless or disfigured spirit and the mutilation of his lower face and mangled jaw was horrifying.

His head was circled in a bandage passing under the chin and tying on top of the head—like the pictures of Jacob Marley in "A Christmas Carol." His arms looked as if they were tied as well and were held rigidly, with his fingers curving unnaturally away from his body. The dead were bound that way for burial in the 19th century. He stared at me with those dead, despairing eyes.

I could hardly bear to look at him. He was so utterly miserable. "Go away, please," I pleaded with him. "Go to the light, please. Just go to the light."

He returned for two more nights, never saying anything, never moving from that rigid corpse-like position—a dead man walking. And on the fourth night, he didn't return.

Historic note: This very lovely hotel is built—foolishly in my opinion—on the site of the Battle of Williamsburg. The central courtyard of the Inn is built around several of the actual earthworks where much of the battle took place in three days of rainy and difficult fighting in 1862.

HOUSES OF HORROR:
Places you wouldn't want to live

Terror in the house does roar
-William Blake-

THE HUNGER

The young woman in the bed stared out the windows at the green fields beyond. Orange lilies flamed around the fences in the June heat but she could only feel the memory of what it had once been like to be warm, to smell the newly-cut hay.

"Has he come yet?" she whispered to the women clustered around her bed. Why do they all wear black? she wondered, feeling the wet heat rise in her throat. Her mother held a basin to her mouth, flinching at the bright torrent of blood. The basin was carried away under a cloth.

"Soon," her mother repeated, smoothing the damp hair back from her daughter's wasted face. "Soon," and the sound melted into the whirring of the doves outside the window....

It was raining as we drove up. The house, set among low, rolling green hills, looked like a miniature Scottish castle—its walls upright, its proportions tall, its windows mullioned. Upstairs, a door led to nowhere. Marks in the stone showed where there had once been a porch. Poppies nodded around the foundation.

Judy King and her husband Steve own the 1792 stone house just outside of Germantown; their friend Sigie Mingie had contacted me and urged me to visit and meet their ghosts.

Judy invited Anne Oscard and I into a low-ceilinged kitchen, immaculately kept, with bright-white walls. Somehow the room reminded me of a cottage kitchen, except that its focal point was not hearth and fireplace, but a TV tuned to *Geraldo*. After introductions, Anne and I did our walkthrough.

The living room was dark, with modern paneling. I was struck with cold looking at the corner where a small door in the paneling led to the upstairs. Off this room was a front parlor, obviously not much used. The bare plaster walls gave the impression of an abandoned house. I don't remember any furniture but I saw a coffin on trestles along one wall.

The entrance hall seemed desolate, cut off, from the warm kitchen at the back of the house. I felt dizzy entering the foyer and hung back. Anne started up the handsome walnut staircase. This is where the young woman ghost has been sighted. She is pathetically thin, made thinner by the black dress she wears, and she holds a handkerchief to her tear-swollen eyes. Sigie, who has seen her, told us, "She always asks, 'Has he come yet?' and cries if you tell her no. Now I just tell her, 'Not yet.'"

The story goes that the young woman starved herself to death, or she may have wasted away from tuberculosis after her husband never returned from the Civil War. Her trembling, shadow-presence was palpable; she was a hunger, a need that could never be satisfied.

At the head of the stairs was a room with a cannonball bed that I could not enter. I have very little sense of smell, but there was a stench in that room—a stench of sickness, decay and death, that had nothing to do with the living world.

Across the hall was a much lighter room with a bed and a sofa covered with toys. Sigie called this the "little girls' room." From her bedroom beneath, Judy has heard her name called and children giggling and jumping up and down on the bed. When Judy's mother lived in the house, she heard someone moving around in that room and assumed that her son and his friend had come in late. She cooked a huge breakfast for the boys, only to find that they weren't there.

Across the entrance hallway was the other parlor, which had been turned into Judy and Steve's bedroom. Judy had tried hard with flowered chintzes and other cheerful accessories, but the room was as gloomy as a crypt. From the bedroom we stepped over a large stone threshhold, like a grave-slab, into a modern bathroom. Judy told us her uncle dropped dead of a heart-attack on that stone threshhold.

We went back into the dark little living room and up the sharply angled staircase with the uneven stairs into the attic area which had been the young woman's quarters. It was hard to believe that anyone had ever lived in these desolate rooms. They were a jumble of boxes and trash; the walls were bare and streaked with damp. There was a sadness, a desolation of spirit as if the young woman's despair had soaked into the walls.

When Judy's mother lived here, she was visited by a former tenant of the house, an elderly lady who told Judy's mother that she used to hear moaning, crying, and the words, "Help me!" coming from the tiny room at the top of the attic stairs.

Back in the kitchen, as we discussed our findings, Judy admitted, "I spend most of my time in the kitchen." She told us about some of the other strange manifestations at the house, which seems to be a veritable way-station for ghosts. Sometimes when one ghost is caught at a site, others are attracted as well.

*Judy and Steve once came upon an old woman sitting in a chair who disappeared when they approached her.

*The couple has heard the sound of carriage doors being opened and shut outside the west entrance to the house, which faced what used to be a bustling county road.

*One night, at 1:15 a.m., a middle shelf in the cupboard dumped all its dishes onto the floor. But when the Kings came down to investigate, they couldn't explain the fact that the cupboard doors were still shut.

*When Judy's parents owned the house, her mother was working outside and saw someone leafing through books at an upstairs window—when the house was supposed to be empty.

Judy's mother also saw lights in the unused upstairs room and heard a baby crying upstairs.

*Judy's sister saw a little boy in old-fashioned clothes and sensed that he had drowned in a well on the property.

*It is said that a man lighting a stove at the top of the stairs, caught his clothes on fire and fell, a tumbling fireball, down the stairs, and out the door where he died in the front yard. Judy and Steve have heard the noise of someone falling down the stairs. His blood still stains the floor by the front door. "It's under the carpet," Judy confirmed, "My mother could never get it clean."

*Judy showed me a photo taken after a ouija board session. I wasn't there and don't know the conditions under which it was taken, but it closely resembles other "spirit" photos I've seen, with smoky streaks like bodies twisting in smoke, one milky mass shaped like a running man, another a gape-mouthed trail of ectoplasm with bulging, blazing eyes.

Records dating back to 1894 show that few of the twenty owners kept the house more than a few years before selling it. It's an unnerving place. I can't imagine trying to live here with the sad young woman, let alone any other spirits. Her hunger for life seemed to devour the house's energy in the way a dying TB victim is suddenly seized with a feverish craving for food.

We left the house, drained.

SHEILA SPOOKS A SPOOK

As I began to write this book, I pulled out my file on Champaign County. There was a story from Julia, postmarked 1995, about a skeletal apparition and a sealed fireplace with bones and strands of red hair inside.

I looked through a few more letters. There was one from Sheila, postmarked 1996: skeletal apparition, sealed fireplace, bones, red hair. Hmmm. Must be fate—which is how I came to include this story told by Julia and her daughter Sheila in this book.

The house was built about 1830 and Julia always felt "watched" there: whenever anyone used the bathroom built beneath the stairs, something walked on the stairs and landing and there was a "cold" room upstairs that was frigid summer or winter. Julia never saw the ghost, but her children did.

Julia said, "My son and his friend were playing in his bedroom, which had a door connecting with Sheila's room. The boys were teasing her through the closed door and she was insulting them back. After a while she quit answering, although they could still hear her moving around in her room. 'Sheila, why aren't you talking?' they called. Finally they went into her room and Sheila wasn't there. The bedcovers had an indentation in it like someone was sitting there. While they watched, the indentation came *up*, as if the person was getting off the bed. They went back into my son's room in a hurry!"

Sheila, who lived in the house until she was 15, had a number of weird experiences.

"My brother and I used to hear a heavy man walking upstairs. You could hear him going, 'thump, thump, thump' You'd think we'd get used to it, but we didn't. We'd run next door to our grandparents' house, even though we weren't supposed to bother them.

"I heard things coming out of the 'cold room.' I was never gutsy enough to look. Once I had a girlfriend spending the night and the next morning she said something about the 'strange things in my room.' She had seen a woman with a long white veil all over her floating at the foot of the bed, just looking at her. It watched her until she drew the covers over her head.

"Normally we didn't walk downstairs in the dark, but one night I needed a drink of water. I turned on the hall light, went down the stairs, through the hallway and into the living room. Just as I turned into the living room, a skeleton *walked* into the room from the kitchen. It looked like a person in a skeleton halloween costume: I could see a black outline around the bones."

The creature's mouth opened and made an "O" of surprise. Then it threw up its hands, startled.

"It jumped. I jumped. We both turned and ran."

Sheila ran to her room where she felt strangely safe, as if she knew she had scared it as badly as it scared her.

The people who bought the house after Julia and her family moved out have denied being visited by ghosts. It's possible that Sheila scared the spooks out of the house, although a macabre discovery may have also laid them to rest. In the course of restoration, the new occupants opened up all of the sealed fireplaces. When they unsealed the one in Sheila's room, they found strands of long red hair, pieces of cloth, and old human bones. No one knows who was burned or bricked up in that fireplace. Perhaps it was enough for the restless spirit that someone finally uncovered its unnatural resting place.

"Ghosts fear men much more than men fear ghosts," goes a Chinese proverb. I wonder if Sheila's timid skeletal intruder ran through the front door and is still running?

FROM DUSK UNTIL MOURNING

During World War II, the rubber factories of Akron were operating at top capacity. Workers flooded into the area to help with the war effort and housing was impossible to find. With a moving van just a day behind, Anne and Jack Wolf took what they could get: an 1860s house on the outskirts of town, originally built by four bricklayer brothers for their mother.

Anne admired the hand-carved black walnut woodwork and staircase and had to admit the house seemed sound, although she wrinkled her nose at the black cobwebs in every corner. The rental agent assured her that they were simply the result of rubber and coal dust in the air. He told them that the last tenants had left suddenly the previous May, having found a farm they liked near Ghent.

Everything else seemed satisfactory and after a massive cleaning bout, the Wolfs moved in. It was a comfortable house and Anne soon had flowering plants in every window. The neighbors and shopkeepers were pleasant, although the grocer refused to open an account for Anne. She put it down to a suspicion of fly-by-night factory workers. When spring came, and the garden burst into blossom, Anne and Jack were delighted with their new home.

On May 24, Anne and Jack lingered over dinner, watching the lights come on in the valley below. Just as Anne poured Jack another cup of tea, there came the sound of feet pounding across the upper floor and down the front steps. A boy's voice called, "Ma! Oh, Ma!"

The renters raced into the living room, but the voice was already beyond the front door. Before Jack could open the door, there came a horrific crash and a series of blood-chilling screams ending in a gurgling choke. Then dead stillness as Jack and Anne swung the door open and looked out into the spring twilight. The air was heavy with the scent of the lilacs flanking the front door; there wasn't a soul in sight.

Behind them, at the head of the stairs, began the sound of uncontrollable weeping.

Jack and Anne crept up the stairs.

"Is any one here?" Jack asked to the dark in the upper hall.

There was no answer. The weeping seemed to come from the master bedroom, but when they looked, it seemed to come from the small back room. They turned on all the upstairs lights and chased the soft, heartbreaking sound from room to room and eventually took flashlights out into the yard. Nothing was there.

It was dawn when the weeping stopped. Exhausted, the couple nodded off on the living room sofa. Jack awoke first, grabbed breakfast, and went off to work. Anne was grateful they hadn't slept in their bed.

"I won't have to go upstairs to make it," she thought, and busied herself with doing the dishes and making out her grocery list. A walk in the fresh air would dispel the nightmare.

As Anne walked down the street, she was too exhausted to notice that every neighbor seemed to be outside, sweeping the porch or sidewalk. Their greetings were eager, even curious, but she was too tired to pay any attention.

The grocer greeted her with "You folks had a party last night! We can see your lights from our house."

Good heavens! she thought. I forgot about the lights we left on. And in the daylight, she felt silly about being so frightened.

At home, Anne put away the groceries and briskly marched upstairs only to get another shock. There, in the bed, the covers were bunched as if a human body lay beneath them. There was a head-sized depression on the pillow. Neither of them had touched the bed last night. No one had been lying on or under it when they had searched before.

Shaken, Anne crept downstairs. When Jack came home, she had dinner waiting and never mentioned the invisible body in the bed. Again the couple watched the lights come on in the valley below. The noises upstairs began again.

The couple poured out more tea and desperately talked of the fine evening weather, of how the lights made the rubber factories seem like a fairyland...

The weeping began and they set down their cups simulta- neously. They began to gather up the dishes, moving quietly, as if in a house where a death had occurred. Then they debated what to do next. The kitchen was the only place they were safe from the invisible mourners.

As they talked, the noises intensified from upstairs and the weeping flowed down the front steps to the front door. Jack and Anne crept towards the dining room and looked towards the front of the house. There was an overpowering stench of flowers, as at a funeral. Not the lilacs, Anne noted mechani- cally. Jack shut the front door. Gagging, they retreated to the kitchen and opened the back door.

Anne's teeth began to chatter from the shock and the chill of the night air as she told Jack about the invisible body in their bed.

"I can't ever sleep in that bed again," she declared. "We might as well give it to the Salvation Army."

"As far as I'm concerned, they can have the house, too," Jack said grimly. "I'm going to see the rental agent first thing in the morning. If we have to, we'll pitch a pup tent in somebody's back yard."

"Jack! Remember the agent told us how every one of the tenants moved out of here in late spring! I'm going to ask the neighbors and the grocer—I'll bet they know what this is about."

The next morning the grocer was eager to share his knowledge:

"Yes, ma'am! Nobody stays in that house past the 24th of May—not since I've been around here, anyway. It seems a good many years ago a big family lived there. All the brothers were bricklayers and they got offers to go to Chicago and help rebuild after the big fire of 1871. All but the youngest. He was 17 or so, a tall, handsome kid and the apple of his mother's eye. He begged to be taken along so he could learn the trade. Finally his mother gave her consent. But she made all the brothers promise they would look out for her baby.

"On the 24th of May, so the story goes—that was his birthday and his mother had him especially in mind—along toward quitting time, this youngest chap was working near the top of a high wall. They were pretty well through and the carpenters were getting the window frames in. Everybody was down off the scaffolding but this youngster. He started down and then remembered a trowel or something. Anyway, he jumped back up, bracing himself on one of the window frames. It wasn't fixed and it gave under his hand, his foot missed the scaffolding and he crashed to the ground and broke his neck. They say he shrieked something awful as he went down!"

"Oh!" gasped Anne. "It must have been just after sun-down."

"Yes. That's another funny angle to it. Just about that time of day his mother was nodding in her chair, you know the way old people do, and suddenly she heard this boy rush down the stairs calling her. He went out the front door and she heard the crash of his body falling. She started to cry something awful and said she knew her baby had been killed. Later the telegram came—and next day his body was brought home, just about dusk."

Suddenly all the noises were explained.

"Nobody ever stays in that house," explained the grocer with relish.

"Why don't they pull it down?"

"Something in the old lady's will. The house that was built for her by her sons is to be a perpetual monument to her baby, or something like that."

Anne and Jack found a brand new house that still smelled of fresh plaster. Nobody had lived—or died—in it yet, which they found reassuring.

The old house was boarded up and Anne and Jack thought that the agent had abandoned the idea of trying to rent it. But a month or so later, they saw carpenters tearing off the front porch and found that the lilacs had been dug up.

In a couple of months, a new family had moved in, complete with young children and a collie romping in the yard.

"Bet they'll have a picnic on May 24th—with a dog in the house," said Jack.

Anne and Jack moved out of Akron before May, but a neighbor wrote to tell them the news: The house was vacant by the middle of summer. She also enclosed a newspaper clipping. Late in May the dog warden and his men shot a mad dog—a collie—in the woods in the valley below the house.[1]

THE PHANTOM HOUSE OF FT. AMANDA

The man in the audience was bearded, intense looking. He smiled knowingly through most of my presentation at Nickleby's Books in Columbus and afterwards approached me with this story. He told me he was an antique dealer from the Lima area. I only took sketchy notes on the story because other fans were waiting in line. I didn't think the details would matter because he had given me the whole story, neatly typed, in a manila envelope.

But that envelope, along with countless other stories disappeared from my office as ghostly stories so often do. I'm reconstructing the story from my notes and apologize to my unknown source. If you recognize yourself—and if you exist in the flesh—please call me.

Built in October of 1812, Fort Amanda was part of a series of forts strung from Piqua to Perrysburg. It served as one of the main supply bases for the American forces during the War of 1812. The 160-foot-square stockade overlooked the Auglaize River where boats were built to ferry supplies to other outposts. No military battles were fought at Ft. Amanda, except those against wounds and disease when the Fort served as a hospital. Now all that is left is a graveyard containing the graves of 75 soldiers, a 50-foot-high granite monument standing in a sea of corn—and one elusive building.

Local residents have reported seeing a phantom house. After a sudden rain shower, Ted* saw a one-story log farmhouse, a building with yellow lights flickering in its windows. It was like "looking through a heat wave" for there were slow flashes of light streaking like elongated fire-flies through the darkness. Ted walked towards the house and it wavered and disappeared. As he trudged back to his car, he found that, oddly, the rain stopped at the highway.

Ted went back the next day. Nothing was there except, of course, the stone monument. He has gone back since and has seen nothing, but others have seen the house—lights flickering cozily in the windows, always on a night when the rain begins out of nowhere.

Perhaps it is a good thing that the house disappears as visitors approach. For anyone mad or daring enough to enter a house from another century that comes and goes so uncertainly might find themselves permanently erased from history.

THE GREEN WOMAN

On North Maple Avenue in Bowling Green, it was known as the neighborhood haunted house. How could it not be when it had been abandoned for over fifty years? Its windows looked down vacantly at the children playing hide-and-seek in its yard, overgrown with weeds and young trees. Its mirrors watched, when Ralph* and his friends found an open window and crawled inside to explore. There they found newspapers with headlines about the assassination of President Garfield and there was no electricity, only candles and oil lamps.

One rainy evening, Ralph, his two brothers, and some of their friends were walking home from a movie. As they passed the house, they looked up at the watching windows. Ralph was the first to see it: somebody standing at the window, pulling back the curtain, then the right shoulder and head of a long-haired woman staring out at them. Only she was glowing green. The only light in the window came from the apparition.

Dumbfounded, the boys stood there for ten or fifteen minutes, then ran home to get Ralph's older brother and sister. When the group returned, the green woman was still there. The longer they stood, trying to figure out what the strange green figure was, the scarier it got. At last they scattered, shivering, to their homes.

The next day the boys went back and looked at the same window. The curtain was back in place, hanging down, as it always had.

Several months later, one rainy night in the fall, the boys were again walking by the mysterious house. There, once again, was the glowing green woman just looking at them, a greenish hand drawing back the curtain.

The next spring, they saw the green image for the third and last time, gazing intently at them. Ralph recalled that what scared him the most was the curtain being pulled back and the fact that they could see facial features green as the mossy skin growing on the tombstones at the cemetery.

When he was fourteen, Ralph, his brother and a friend, went into the house to try to solve the mystery of the apparition that so many of his friends and neighbors had witnessed. The house was like a time machine. It was filled with Victorian furniture, walnut desks and tables, an oriental rug on the floor, beautiful oil lamps. The place was like a museum, except that everything was covered in a thick shroud of dust.

Upstairs, in the front room where they had seen the apparition, they found the window open just a crack, enough to let in dust, dirt, and rain. But the room was clean, as if someone or something had been keeping it up. The bed's covers were turned down as if somebody had just left—or someone was expected.

The boys hoped to find a mannequin or something that had deceived them into thinking they'd seen a woman, but there was nothing at all near the window. The curtains hung primly straight. There were no smudges on the glass that could have been mistaken for a person.

The atmosphere in the room was uneasy, as if they had roused something that didn't want to be wakened. They looked back over their shoulders as they quietly crept down the stairs. To this day, none of them can explain the strange glowing green woman they saw at the window, staring at them as if to sear an image of the living in her memory—she who had perhaps forgotten what it was like to be alive.[2]

HOUSE OF BONES

Bones we are and to bones we shall return. Even a skeleton lying still and gape-jawed in its grave can arouse in us the terror of death. And the idea of a *living* skeleton is almost too terrifying to be borne.

In the mid-1920s, Susan* and her parents lived in a big old house in Trumbull County. It was rather isolated and there were no other kids her age except for Evelyn, a girl from the farm next door. When Evelyn came over on one of her rare visits, the girls would go to the sealed-off upstairs bedrooms to hold tea parties or play hide-and-seek.

On this particular day Evelyn was doing the hiding. She ducked into a closet, the door was screened by a calico curtain, and waited for Susan to find her. Susan found her friend quickly, flinging aside the curtain triumphantly. Then Evelyn saw Susan's expression change to terror.

"C'mere quick!" Susan shrieked, dragging Evelyn out of the closet by her hand. Evelyn turned to see a skeleton, an animated, *moving* skeleton, bouncing up and down as if on a rope. It grinned at them and they fled in hysterics. Susan had seen the skeleton looming over Evelyn, stretching out its bony fingers for her neck.

Besides the "skeleton in the closet," the house was strangely alive in other ways. Susan hated and feared the cellar, which was full of disembodied eyes floating in the dark, watching her, unwinking, whenever she was sent into the unlit root cellar.

Bizarre eyes haunted another room of the house as well. Susan's father had been a member of a polar expedition when he was younger. Wildlife laws weren't as strict then and he'd brought back a polar bear skull which was mounted on a wooden shield plaque in the living room. The beast had been turned into a timepiece: the jaws had been spring-loaded and an alarm clock wedged in among the massive teeth. One evening, Susan was doing her homework at the living room table while her parents read the newspaper. She heard a click and looked up to find a bone-chilling horror.

The polar bear's skull had living *eyes* in its empty sockets. The pale blue eyes rolled wildly, sometimes focusing on *her*. Then the jaw began to chatter.

"Maw!" Susan yelled, "Look!"

Her parents looked. They both saw the living eyes in the dead eye sockets. The jaw chattered and champed until the clock fell out. Then the eyes melted away and the skull was still and dead again.

HAUNTED HIGHWAYS:
Highway and transport ghosts

Death's road we all must go.
-Horace-

One of the first stories I heard when I started researching the *Haunted Ohio* series was that Carpenter Road in Greene County was haunted. By what, nobody could say specifically, although later I heard various tales of ghostly tractors and one with a madwoman who lived in a house at the bend of the road, seen staring out the window after her death. Then I met a man after giving a talk at a local library.

"You know Carpenter Road in Beavercreek?" he asked me.

"Of course!" I said, "Which story do you know?"

He smiled. "Actually, it's about what me and a buddy did. There was this house at the bend in the road where this old woman had lived. We broke in and put a department store mannequin in the window. It was still there, last time we checked..."

Another ghost sighting explained. But not all of these tales of highways from hell have such a simple solution...

THE PHANTOM DRIVER OF OLD 40

I've always found the stretch of Old U.S. 40 by Englewood Dam a lonely and unnerving place. Back in the 1950s, it was a real nightmare for truck drivers, especially in icy winter weather. The narrow road over the Taylorsville and Englewood Dams was protected only by a wooden rail and any mistake might send a big rig and its driver plunging 125 feet to certain death.

Near the west end of the Englewood Dam was a truckstop. One freezing night in the winter of 1952, a driver named Roy Fitzwater came staggering into the inn. The other drivers looked him over. Many there knew him. He was an experienced driver, approaching middle age, and usually calm and collected. But tonight he was as pale as a ghost.

"Not feeling well?" a friend asked.

"I'm not sick," Fitzwater said shortly.

"What's wrong?" pressed his friend.

But all Fitzwater would say was, "Something—strange— happened out there." He lapsed into an uncharacteristic silence over his sandwich and coffee, eating rapidly, with the set stare of someone playing something over and over in his mind.

Highway Patrolman Harrell was also at the truck stop that night. He had met Fitzwater before and knew him to be a stable, conscientious driver who never touched a drop while driving. But tonight Fitzwater was a nervous wreck. Harrell strolled over and took the stool next to the driver.

"Hey, buddy, anything I can do?" Harrell asked.

Fitzwater shook his head. "I'd rather not talk about it."

"You sure? Sometimes it helps just to get things off your chest."

Fitzwater blinked and turned his head abruptly to look at the patrolman. His eyes were opened a little too wide, with an unnerving show of whites, like a spooked horse.

"All the fellows here would just laugh if I told you, but it was something—horrible."

With that, he gulped the rest of his coffee, threw a half-dollar on the counter, and left the inn with everyone staring after him.

Several days after this, Patrolman Harrell had again stopped at the inn for a cup of coffee. He hadn't been there very long before another driver entered. He was a hearty-looking sort in a red plaid shirt, but he was dead-pale. Harrell watched as he ordered coffee, then spilled half of it down his front. The man's hand shook wildly.

His fellow drivers saw this and teased him: "Hey, Bud, whatsamatter? What's giving you the shakes?"

The driver shook his head. "I don't want to talk about it." he said, carefully putting his cup down, then pressing his hand over it, white-knuckled, to keep it from shaking. "None of you guys would believe it anyway." He, too, left the inn quickly.

A week later, a third driver came into the inn displaying the same symptoms; then a few days later, a fourth man. Harrell questioned each of them in a friendly way, but got nowhere: "Forget it, Officer," they'd say, avoiding his eyes. "You wouldn't believe me." They would flee into the dark to their trucks.

Harrell puzzled over this mystery. All of the men had been going west and he deduced that they had seen something on or near the Englewood Dam that totally unnerved them. It couldn't be the narrow, icy roads; these truck drivers were used to conditions like those all along the National Road. Whatever it was only affected those who drove the big rigs. Patrolman Harrell decided that the fifth driver who came in on his watch would tell him the truth about the matter, even if he had to threaten to arrest him on some technicality!

A week after Harrell spoke to the fourth driver, the officer was having his dinner at the inn when Roy Fitzwater staggered in. His face was white and drawn and he looked as if he was about to collapse. Harrell muscled him into a chair and waited until the man had stopped shivering. After his third cup of coffee, Harrell leaned over and said,

"Since you came in a month ago, I've met three other drivers in the same state as you. You've got to tell me: what is it?"

Fitzwater bit his lip, then said, "All right. Since you've met other guys like me, I guess I can't be crazy, can I? That's why I wouldn't talk before; what I saw was so horrible, I couldn't believe I was really seeing it. I wasn't drunk, but normal people don't see the—thing—I saw. I thought I was having hallucinations. I didn't want to talk about it because everybody would have said I was nuts!"

"What did you see?"

"I was headed west on 40 and about the middle of the dam, I see a car turn onto the bridge at the other end and come straight at me, lights on high, blinding me. He looked like he wanted to play chicken and force me off the dam. I stood on the brakes, and swerved, knowing I only had a little room to maneuver or I'd go through the rail and over the edge.

"About 200 feet from me, the car swerved to the right and its headlights went out. But another light was inside the car. It was a ghastly blue-green light, like the sky gets before a bad storm, and I swear to God there was a skeleton driving that car, its bones all lit up in that horrible light and its greenish teeth grinning at me!"

Fitzwater covered his face with his hands.

"You don't know what it does to a man, seeing something like that. It takes the life right out of you, knowing either that you're losing your mind or, worse yet, something like that is real."

Harrell laid a hand on Fitzwater's shoulder. "You're not losing your mind; the other drivers must have seen it too. I'll do my best to track down the idiot playing this stupid trick."

Many patrolmen were put on watch to find the perpetrator. But no earthly perpetrator was ever found. When spring came, there were no more reports of the phantom driver, nor were there any the following winter or since.[1]

THE GHOST TRAIN OF REPUBLIC

It was January of 1887 and a bad blizzard had blown up, reducing visibility along the train tracks to less than a quarter mile. A freight train carrying barrel hoops, was racing to reach the safety of a siding before Chicago Limited Express train No. 5 came through. The freight engine left the station with 30 pounds of steam; it wasn't enough and the train died on the incline about a mile and a half outside of Republic, in Seneca County. The frantic conductor ran with his lantern to try to head off the Chicago passenger train, but No. 5 collided head-on with the freight train at 50 miles an hour. The wooden cars telescoped, trapping many people in the wreckage. And then the fires broke out.

Sixteen people burned to death as rescuers looked on helplessly. Eventually the unclaimed and unidentifiable bodies were buried in a common grave in nearby Farewell Retreat Cemetery. Then the rumors began that at night you could see the passenger train steaming down the tracks to her doom.

To Reb* these weren't just idle rumors.

"Between the ages of 12 to 16, I spent a lot of time in the woods east of Republic, behind the cemetery. One summer, my two cousins came up from southern Ohio to stay a couple of weeks. We had our camp set up behind the piney woods.

"It was maybe one in the morning. Me and Terry, a buddy of mine, were sitting around the campfire while my cousins were asleep in the tent. Our camp was only about 50 feet from the tracks, close enough to feel the rumble of any passing train. We heard a train whistle. The crossing was only about a mile and a half east of where we were. Usually you'd hear the train whistle at the crossing and the train'd be on top of you in a couple of minutes. But this time it seemed like it took forever. We'd sat there for a half hour and began to wonder why the train didn't come.

"This got us curious and we walked out of the woods and up to the tracks. We saw a light way down at the corner. I swear that damn thing was waiting for us to come out. Then we could see the light coming down the tracks. It wasn't bright like a regular train light, but white and glowing. It was floating, kind of bobbing up and down in a wave motion. I thought maybe it was coon hunters with their headlights on, walking down the tracks, but the light was up way too high for that.

"We got off the tracks and crouched down below in some bushes to avoid getting shot at, if it *was* hunters. Then it came. We could see it go by. It was noisy and the wind swept by me. I could smell the coal and the smoke. When I first saw it, I thought it was a real train. Maybe a bicentennial thing like when they get old engines out of mothballs sometimes and run them. Then I realized I could see through the damn thing...

"I could see the trees on the other side of the track. The cars were lit up, but I don't remember any people. I remember the curtains with fringes in the windows. Terry also said he could see the trees on the other side too and he could smell the smoke. It seemed like it took forever to pass. We hopped on the tracks afterwards, less than three seconds later. We couldn't see the train or the light; we couldn't feel any wind. There was nothing there.

"We woke up my cousins; they thought we were nuts. Terry and I stayed up a few more hours, trying to convince ourselves we did see what we saw. No, we weren't scared— we were teenagers: nothing could kill us!

"Me and Terry kept this to ourselves for a long time. Down at Rock Creek, I found two pairs of old wire-rim glasses. There are people in town who have watches and things from the wreck. I'd like to see the train again, maybe try to flag it down. But ride on it? Not possible! There's only one way you could get on that train...."

GET ME TO THE CHURCH ON TIME

Trebein Road near Byron in Greene County is an isolated roller-coaster of a road. Softly rolling hills make it impossible to see more than the next hill ahead, from the top of each rise. Oncoming cars rise sharply out of the dips and valleys. On this road, you cannot see where you have been or where you are going; there is only the present.

And it is always the Present for the ghostly veiled woman in white who crosses Trebein Road. You may catch a glimpse of her in your headlights as you top a rise, but once your car dives into the spot—she has vanished like the fog that melts beneath your high beams.

Some witnesses have described the lady as vaporous, shadowlike, ethereal. But most say she looks as real as a living person, so real, some witnesses have stopped their cars and gone in search of the vision in white.

Before Fairfield and Osborn merged to form the town of Fairborn, a prominent family farmed along Trebein Road. The daughter of the family was engaged to marry an Osborn man. For weeks, her mother and aunts pinned, stitched, and fussed over altering and fitting the girl's wedding dress, which had been her grandmother's. At last it fit perfectly.

On the wedding day, the household was in a flurry of preparations. The mother, brother, and sister went early to decorate the church. It was agreed that when the girl finished dressing, her father would take her to town in the buckboard.

The horse stamped, jingling its harness as it waited for the young bride. Finally, looking lovely, she climbed into the buggy—at the very time she should have been at the church. As the bride and her father pulled onto dusty Trebein Road, she urged him to make up the lost time. He snapped the whip and the horse broke into a fast canter. The bride's cheeks were pink with excitement as she held her flower circlet in place while her veil billowed out behind.

The road was no smoother then than it is now and the buckboard bottomed out in a dip of the road just as one wheel hit a rock. The sprung seat acted like a catapult, flinging the bride out into the dust. She fell like a rag doll stuffed with sawdust, her neck broken. Dressed in her grandmother's bridal gown, she was buried two days later at a little cemetery on Byron Road, less than a mile as the crow flies from where the accident happened.

The day before the funeral, the distraught father and the grieving groom dug the rock out of the road and filled the hole. The rock turned out to be about the size of a bushel basket. They rolled it into the ditch nearby where it remains today.

No one can say when you will see the bride in white crossing Trebein. Some say she wanders on the anniversary of her death, her wedding or her funeral. Some say on her birthday, or the night her fiance proposed. But all versions agree that she is trying to get to the church—better late than never.[2]

THE ERIE SPIRITS OF THE *SUCCESS*

It is a long trip from Australia to Cleveland, a longer passage from the 18th to the 20th century, and the longest journey of all for spirits that cannot rest. This is the story of the unending voyage of the *Success*.

It was 1790. The sun had just barely risen on the British Empire. Built to make an impression in the ports of the Far East, the luxurious barkentine *Success* was the finest ship British money could buy. Her timbers were Burmese teak; her ballast Indian marble. Her brass cannon could fend off China Sea pirates or fire a salute to a native prince invited to dinner with the captain.

It is not known whether *The Success* ever made a good impression on the nabobs. Perhaps even then, she bore some taint, some ocean-going curse, for it is a curious thing that such a luxurious vessel should be converted to a prison ship as early as 1802, only 12 years after being commissioned. Her facilities for entertaining were turned to unpleasant accommodations for a very different type of guest.

For years, the *Success* transported British convicts to the dreaded penal colonies of Australia. She might as well have been a slave ship with her cramped iron cages, foul air, maggot-infested food, and filthy, overcrowded cells. Each voyage was a horror and only the strongest survived.

Eventually the *Success* was anchored in Sydney harbor as a prison ship. Among the prisoners sealed below her hatches was an Irishman named Harry Power, sentenced to 14 years for poaching. He had spent half his sentence in mind-rotting solitary confinement.

The rat-infested ship was scuttled in 1885, but was raised again five years later. Some promoters, correctly reading the tastes of the public, thought that her evil reputation would make her a popular attraction. She was refitted with iron cages, whips, and manacles, and, to add a realistic touch, wax figures of some of the most notorious inmates. One was Harry Power, chained in his solitary cell.

Power had served his full sentence and been freed, but he was old and poor with no way to make a living. Ironically, Power was hired as a guide on his former prison ship as it toured Australian ports. We can only wonder what he relived every time he pointed out his own wax figure to sticky-fingered children and their avid parents. Walking by that likeness must have been like meeting his own dreadful double in the dark, a ghost of his former self. One day Power couldn't bear the painful memories any more; he threw himself overboard.

Searching for new audiences, *Success's* owners took their horror show to the British Isles for several years of lucrative touring, then set their sights on North America. Crossing the Atlantic, the crew complained of weird noises at night and refused to work below deck. Some said they had seen ghostly arms reaching from the cells, most notably from the one where Harry Power had rotted alone.

After a nightmarish voyage, the *Success* reached American shores and earned money for her owners in Boston, New York, Philadelphia and San Francisco. No longer able to sail under her own power, the venerable ship was towed up the St. Lawrence to the Great Lakes and a new audience. She was a popular attraction for many years, and a favorite at the Great Lakes Exposition of 1936 in Cleveland. Who could tell what stories were locked in her ancient timbers, what ghostly crews and cargo came to life in the late watches of the night?

However, time was running out for the ancient ship. In 1946, the *Success* was destroyed in a storm on Lake Erie and the wreck was torched by vandals. It is said that as she burned, the ghosts of a thousand convicts, finally freed from torment, rose above the flames, and fled into the darkness—perhaps to Heaven, or to join the legion of lost souls haunting the Great Lakes.[3]

THE SPECTRAL SEDAN

Herb was sitting in the catbird seat, or perhaps we should say, the Studebaker seat. It was 1949. He was young, it was a bright sunny fall day, and he was being paid to do something he really enjoyed: drive.

Herb was a deliveryman for Cleveland Laboratories, ferrying dentures and glasses in the company car from the Lab to doctors in the Cleveland suburbs.

The 1947 Studebaker handled like a dream as he approached Cleveland from the west side, Herb drove east on Lake Avenue, hitting all the green lights. Right on schedule, he thought with satisfaction. There was only one more light before he could hop on the main road to downtown. As he approached, the light turned yellow. Herb floored it and the Studebaker zipped through the intersection just as the light turned red.

He was still barreling along when a black sedan pulled out of the next street almost directly in front of him. The black car poked along, barely going 35 miles an hour. Irritated, Herb hit the brakes—only to find that he had no brakes. He pumped the brake pedal, but he might as well have been tuning the radio for all the good it did. Worse, the black sedan stopped at the next intersection, waiting for oncoming traffic to clear so it could turn left. The Studebaker rumbled towards it. There was no place for Herb to go. He couldn't veer left into the traffic. The curb was lined with parked cars and there wasn't room between them and the black sedan for even a bicycle to pass.

Horrified, Herb saw a woman and a young girl in the front seat of the sedan. He laid on the horn, but they ignored him completely. Seconds away from collision, Herb decided to ram the parked cars. But it was too late. His car was moving too fast. He braced himself on the steering wheel for the impact— for the scream of tearing metal, for the shattering of glass. His stomach rose in his throat.

For a split second the street went dark, a greenish darkness. Herb could see the outline of the front hood of his car penetrating the dark trunk of the sedan.

There was no sound and the two people in the front seat did not move or even flinch. Then they disappeared. Herb felt like he was floating through a greenish murk, his hands still glued to the steering wheel. He had the bizarre sensation of passing right through the other car.

The darkness abruptly changed back to the bright daylight. As Herb glanced into his rearview mirror, he was astounded to see the black sedan still waiting in the same spot. But now it was behind him. How could that be?

As soon as traffic cleared, the mysterious black sedan completed its turn and drove down a side street with both occupants staring straight ahead, completely ignoring Herb, as if he didn't exist, as if nothing had happened. He desperately wanted to follow the car, but he was still struggling helplessly to control the Studebaker without brakes.

The next block had no cars parked along its curb and by steering next to the curb, he was able to stop the runaway Studebaker. He shut off the engine and put his head in his hands, moaning, "My God! What happened back there?" He knew he wasn't traveling fast enough to fly over the top of the mysterious sedan. He certainly hadn't gone under it, and there wasn't enough room to go around it. Had he really gone *through* it?

Herb climbed slowly out of the Studebaker, staring back down the street, trying to spot that black sedan. His legs were shaking so much he nearly collapsed. A friendly woman let him use her phone to call a tow truck.

"So, what happened to your car?" asked the driver. Herb started to say that he had just driven through a car, but he could tell that the driver would think he was a loony. Better keep quiet.

"My brakes failed," said Herb.

As the tow truck pulled onto the road, it was enveloped by the usual midday traffic jam. Herb shuddered: What would have happened a half-hour earlier if he had come charging up that road in a car that had no brakes?

The phantom black sedan, with its indifferent passengers, had just saved his life and the lives of how many others?[4]

AND WE WERE DRIVING, DRIVING IN YOUR CAR

It was three a.m. Things were pretty quiet around Urbana:
all the fights were over and there were few cars on the streets.
As they drove their police cruiser by Urbana High School,
Officer Brian Cordial and his partner Dave Reese noticed a car
parked on the east side of the school. There didn't seem to be
anyone in the car, but they pulled up behind it. Brian told Dave
to radio dispatch their location and run a stolen-vehicle check.

"As I was talking to Dave, I could see in the passenger's
side mirror, a young teenage girl with long, straight light-
colored hair and a thin build ducking down as if attempting to
hide from the cruiser. I knew she was looking at me because
the two of us made direct eye contact.

"I told Dave there was a girl in the car and that I would go
check the girl and send her on her way."

Brian got out of the cruiser slowly. Police officers know
that routine traffic stops are one of the most dangerous parts of
their job. Brian assumed the worst he was going to find was an
entangled teenaged couple, but he walked carefully as he
approached the passenger side of the car. "I figured the girl was
just a local kid out with her boyfriend, ducking down in the
driver's seat."

A few more steps and Brian shone his flashlight into the
car. He couldn't believe what he saw: the car was empty.

"I did a double take. I *knew* I had seen somebody in that
mirror. There wasn't anyone at all in the car. I stepped back,
confused. I walked slowly around the back of the car and back
to the passenger side. I still didn't see anyone in the car. But I
could still see her in the mirror, looking right at me! Her
expression was like, 'Oh, gosh, here come the police!' I shined
my light in the car again. Nothing. It spooked me."

Dave radioed in the out-of-county license plate. There was
no problem, the car wasn't stolen; there were no warrants out
for the owner. Dave saw Brian walking slowly around the car
and back to the passenger side and he wondered why Brian was
acting so funny, why he wasn't talking to the girl.

Dave got out of the cruiser. "What are you doing, man?" he asked Brian who seemed extremely jittery.

"Stand right there," Brian told Dave. "Just tell me what you see in that car. Look at the passenger-side mirror." Brian could still see the girl in the mirror, looking at them. He wondered if Dave saw her too or were his eyes playing tricks on him?.

Dave looked. "Brian, there's a girl in there! Go back to the car and tell her to get on her way."

"What does she look like?" Brian wanted to confirm that Dave was seeing what he was seeing.

"Thin, long blonde hair, just a kid."

"I see her too, but, man, there is *nobody* in that car," Brian said.

They went back to the cruiser. "There she was again," Dave recalled, "looking at us. It knocked me for a loop. She was young and had blonde hair. There was nothing real distinguished about her. All I could make out was a face."

Later Brian told me, "We got back in our cruiser and got out of there. Knowing that there was no one in the car, we sped away from the school and we never went back that night. The next day the car was gone."

Dave said, "I've often thought about it. We checked so many cars on that shift that it would be hard to find that particular one. But it wasn't stolen. There was nothing strange about it in the computer. "After that we went straight to my house and sat there for a long time. It spooked both of us. Brian said he thought we saw a ghost. It was real plain. I don't know what it was. I looked in there. The car was locked, but there were no blankets or anything that people could have been hiding under."

Traditional ghostlore says that ghosts are often visible in mirrors. Was the blonde girl a murdered runaway? An accident victim? Or, possibly, a phantom hitchhiker, just along for the ride.

YOU ALWAYS HAUNT
THE ONE YOU LOVE:
Ghostly relatives

*There is a land of the living and there is a land
of the dead, and the bridge is love.*
-Thornton Wilder-

Some of the most common ghost stories I encounter are
about the ghost of a family member. Even the most skeptical
people will tell me thoughtfully, "Well, something strange *did*
happen after Uncle Fred died..." Family ties are not easily
severed, even by death.

HELEN

Helen loved the old maple tree out behind her Clarksburg
farmhouse in southern Pickaway County. She would sit under
it, peeling potatoes, shelling peas, or just reading a book,
enjoying the breeze. Sometimes when her grandbabies came
for a visit, she would sit serenely snapping beans as they
tumbled about in the long, cool grass.

Helen passed away in January of 1988. That spring, as her
son Charles was ploughing her small farm field, he automatically glanced up at the house. There he saw his mother
standing under her favorite maple tree. She wore the old
pastel-print housedress and broad-brimmed straw hat she'd
always worn when she worked in the garden. She smiled and
waved at him like she always did to tell him lunch was ready.

It was a bright, clear day. Charles froze where he was.
His mother was too far away to call out to, and Charles was

afraid if he got down off the tractor and started towards the house, she would disappear. He didn't want to look away for even a moment, so he just turned off the tractor and sat there watching her. Overcome by her presence, he could not take his eyes off her.

She waved several times, smiled a lot, and took her hat off. Then a loud pickup truck coming down the road distracted him and he glanced away just for a second. To his great disappointment, when he looked back, she was gone. He had longed so much to see her again, enjoy her loving smile just one more time. Now, whenever he is at the farm, he automatically glances at that tree. And though he always sees his mother in his memory, she has never appeared again.

THE LAST LAUGH

Gayle K. Lewis of Swanton sent me this delightful Fulton County story about a *living* mother who decided to spook her kids.

One dark October morning, close to Halloween, my children, Dustin and Mindy and I sat in our car at the end of our driveway waiting for the school bus. Across the road and to our left, stood a big vacant farmhouse. The previous tenant, Mrs. Cook*, had been dead for several years and the house now belonged to her son John*.

This weatherbeaten old house had been John's childhood home and he would have liked nothing better than to fix it up and move in. But his wife didn't like the isolated rural setting, so they continued to live in town. John couldn't bring himself to part with his boyhood home so he kept it and periodically he came out to cut the grass and tinker around the place. He and his wife never stayed overnight in the house.

On this particular morning, I noticed a light in the back bathroom of John's farmhouse. We viewed the house every morning while we waited for the bus, but I had never noticed any lights before. It was then that I decided to have some Halloween fun with my kids. I pointed out the light and began

to spin a ghostly tale about good old Mrs. Cook coming back
for one last Halloween prank. Mrs. Cook was a sweet old lady,
full of fun and childlike mischief and she loved playing tricks!

My children didn't buy it. They said that the light was
probably left on for security or John simply forgot to turn it out
the last time he was there. I pretended to be skeptical so my
daughter played along. "Boy, Mom, I bet you'd have a heart
attack if that light suddenly went off..." she teased.

We were joking about the possibility, when, just seconds
later, the light went out!

I shivered. What started out as a joke to spook my kids
was now starting to spook me too!

"John must have put a timer on the light in the bathroom
so it would appear that someone was living there...that's all it
is. We just never noticed it before," I said.

All three of us sat quietly for a moment. There seemed to
be another light coming from another room near the front of the
house. *Two* timers, I thought desperately, in *two* different
rooms?

That seemed logical and my fear subsided. I decided to
carry the joke a step further. In my best spooky voice I said,
"Someone's in there... Maybe it's Mrs. Cook... Let's go knock
on the door and see who answers."

Lucky for me, neither of my kids was willing to walk up to
that door. But Dustin was curious enough to challenge me to
drive over to see if anyone was there. He was confident that
John had gotten off work early from his night-shift job and we
would surely see his car parked in the drive. No big deal.
Nothing to be afraid of....

Now, I'm not a mean mother, but I saw my chance to play
a harmless, yet successful Halloween prank on my kids. After
all, that's what Halloween is all about to me: being scared by
something that isn't so scary once you know what it really is.

I played my final card. Both kids were already on edge.
I'd drive over to Mrs. Cook's. We'd sit silently in the dark,
building up the suspense and, then, when they least expected it,
I'd scream, "BOO!" It was perfect! No one would get hurt and

we'd all have a good laugh about how we'd spooked each other.

With a slight pang of conscience, I approached the driveway. There was no car in the drive. John wasn't there. We crept up the drive and stopped parallel with the living room picture window. A soft glow of light shown dimly from inside. I was just about to turn off the headlights when Dustin shouted, "Look! There's someone in there!"

Standing just beyond the filmy white curtains was the outline of a woman wearing what appeared to be a long robe! I couldn't believe my eyes!

I fumbled for the gearshift and ground the car into reverse. As I made my hasty retreat, I could see the woman inside move closer to the window, trying to see her unexpected visitors!

But we weren't waiting around to see who she was or if, in fact, she was Mrs. Cook. We were getting out of there— FAST!

To this day, none of the neighbors has ever known John or his wife to stay in that house overnight. Nor have we seen lights in it since that morning in October.

I wonder if good old Mrs. Cook got the last laugh after all? I'd like to think so. She would have liked that.

AN OBSESSION WITH AMANDA

On the west corner of Muskingum and Market Streets, in the shadow of the United Presbyterian Church, stood a handsome but rather forlorn brick house. It was built in 1876 by a Cadiz attorney named John Stoneman Pearce. In its time, the house was a village showplace where Colonel Pearce, a much-honored veteran of the Civil War, regularly received and entertained friends. After the deaths of Col. Pearce and his wife Emma, the house was home to a succession of families until a few years ago. Since then it stood deserted and decaying until it was torn down.

The mystery surrounding the house began in the spring of 1975. Mrs. Aiken* came to Cadiz from Cleveland with her husband on a business trip. While he went to his appointment, she strolled through the courthouse grounds, crossed the village square and walked toward the Christian Church on North Main Street. As she approached the church, some strange urge made her do an about-face and hurry in the opposite direction.

At the town square she turned abruptly west and strode along Market Street to the corner of Muskingum. There she paused for breath, wondering what strange force had directed her there. Suddenly she saw Pearce House across the street. It was love—or obsession—at first sight.

She crossed the street and circled the house several times. She peered in at the dirty windows, trying to catch a glimpse of the darkened rooms. She could see little, but she had the terrifying feeling that somebody inside wanted desperately to speak to her. Frightened by the unknown force drawing her to the house, she broke away and returned to her car. They left town later that day, but she knew she would be back.

Indeed, a week later, Mrs. Aiken came back to Cadiz. She searched the library and the county recorder's office for information on the house. She wanted to buy the house, she said. But facts and figures paled as she again walked around Pearce House. The yearning feeling was still there—someone or something shut up inside, calling out, reaching out to her.

On her next visit, Mrs. Aiken went boldly up to the door of Pearce House and tried the knob. To her disappointment, it was locked. As she stood there puzzling over her next move, she saw the ivy surrounding the door begin to stir and slither. It extended one stiff tendril like a bony finger into the keyhole, and clicked open the lock.

Her judgment entirely at the mercy of her obsession, Mrs. Aiken stepped inside. The foyer was dim and smelled of mildew and dust. But it was alive with a female presence so strong Mrs. Aiken could almost see it move through the stale air. This presence was trying to talk. The "voice" was like fragments of a radio show heard through static. Yet, gradually, Mrs. Aiken began to understand.

The spirit wanted the house restored. She was adamant. The spirit's name seemed to be Amelia, but when Mrs. Aiken spoke the name out loud, a shockwave rippled through the house. Then the spirit disappeared and Mrs. Aiken, utterly disconcerted by the ivy, and the presence, and the "voice," left the house. Behind her, the door lock snapped back into place.

Mrs. Aiken believed that Pearce House had been the home of Congressman John A. Bingham. But her research showed that Bingham had never owned the house, nor had he lived there. Stubbornly, she clung to the idea that there was *some* connection. Bingham's wife's name had been Amanda—could she have mis-heard this as "Amelia"?

The next weekend Mrs. Aiken again arrived at Pearce House and was again let in by the same mysterious force. Again, the female presence hovered in the hall. Mrs. Aiken greeted her as "Amanda." At that, the spirit happily began to talk to Mrs. Aiken. "Amanda" had spent "many happy hours" in Pearce House when the Congressman had been away on business because her own house was "so lonely," she said. She also said that she wanted Pearce House restored because she now had "no home of her own."

Mrs. Aiken was convinced that this was indeed the spirit of Amanda Bingham and returned to Cleveland, ready to raise the money to restore the house to its previous glories. Instead she found an irate husband, incensed over her mysterious trips to Cadiz and her suspicious number of long-distance phone calls. Mrs. Aiken has never returned to Pearce House.

Was this just the hallucination of a woman with a too-vivid imagination? Or did Mrs. Aiken actually encounter the spirit of Amanda Bingham? Local townspeople didn't know what to think, particularly after she told them about the ivy. Why would Amanda Bingham be so excited about a house she never even owned?

Not long afterwards, some of the people who helped Mrs. Aiken research the home in Cadiz realized that she may have been right about several things. When Amanda told the lady that she had "no home of her own," she was telling the literal truth. The Bingham house, which had stood at the very spot where Mrs. Aiken was "compelled" to change course on North

Main Street, burned down in December, 1963. In 1975, it was
only a memory.

Amanda had indeed spent "many happy hours" at Pearce
House. According to contemporary newspapers reports, both
John and Amanda visited there often, sometimes for days at a
time and Amanda frequently stayed there while John was in
Washington. Why? Emma Pearce was Amanda Bingham's
sister. Amanda was seeking a family reunion, beyond the
grave.[1]

DUSTY

Vivian has a peaches-and-cream complexion and radiant
blonde hair. She possesses a sweetness of personality rarely
met with in this world and she immediately made me feel like
one of the family at the Marion Meijer store where I was doing
a book signing. Several members of her family have died in
the last few years, but she knows they are still with her. Here
are some of her stories.

My husband drives a semi and right after I lost my father-
in-law, I was up late getting my work done so I could go out
with him for a few days. As I put the dishes in the dishwasher, I
heard my father-in-law's voice say, "Watcha doin'?"

Without thinking, I said, "Doin' dishes."

I just stopped dead in my tracks. I turned around, *knowing*
he was going to be right behind me. Nobody was there.

I walked to the bedroom door, thinking maybe it had been
my husband, but he was sound asleep. Besides, it wasn't his
voice; it was my father-in-law's voice. He used to visit every
day; I'd fix him hot chocolate; we'd sit and talk. And the first
words out of his mouth were always, "Watcha doin'?"

Back when my mother-in-law and father-in-law lived in a
house near us, Dusty, my pet Pomeranian would run over there;
it was just a quarter of a mile up the road. He was black, very
small, with a big tail that curled over his back. After my
father-in-law died, Dusty still went to visit my mother-in-law.

She'd call him: "Here, Dusty, Dusty!" and he'd go and she'd feed him. He was good company for her.

My mother-in-law died in 1987 and in the spring of 1988, I found Dusty dying in our front yard. He must have been hit by a car or something. Poor Dusty didn't last long.

We rented my mother-in-law's house out to a family and one day the man asked me, "Do you have any neighbors around here who have a dog named Dusty? I got up in the middle of the night to use the bathroom and I heard a woman calling 'Here, Dusty, here Dusty.'"

I told him that the dog did belong to me, "but he's no longer here." Then I told him how my mother-in-law had lived in house, and used to call the dog and feed him. That really got to him!

SHE CAME BACK TO SAY GOODBYE

The Italians believe that the dead come back to say goodbye to the ones who loved them the most. Suzanne came back to her cousin Angela in the summer of 1973.

"She was the sweetest thing," Angela said, "I think about her every day. But she was like a lost soul on this earth."

Suzanne died in April, 1973 as a result of an epileptic seizure. Her bed stood against the bedroom wall and on many nights she would strike her head against the wall during a seizure. The family had actually gotten used to the noise because it usually stopped within a few seconds and Suzanne would recover. Only this particular night, Suzanne hit her head so hard that she died. She was only nineteen.

In all honesty, Angela was not completely sad Suzanne was dead; she was glad that she had gone on to a better life. Her aunts and uncles were relieved too; one uncle said to Angela, "Well, we don't have to listen to her anymore."

Suzanne had been classed as a "slow learner." Few of her relatives enjoyed being with her because she was intensely curious and would pester them by repeating questions she had just asked.

"I liked being around her because Suzanne longed to be 'normal' and I tried to encourage her to do things, like the time she volunteered to count Grandma's canning jars. She struggled laboriously for minutes, then was off by one, but I let her report to Grandma. She was so proud of herself!"

She was buried on the outskirts of Bettsville, down the road from Carey, in her favorite rose-pattern dress with the puffed sleeves.

It was a hot summer night when Suzanne appeared to Angela—just a figure in a coat with "Bettsville High School" on the back, standing on the sidewalk in front of Angela's home in Tiffin.

"For a moment I thought it was Suzanne's sister, Jeannie, and asked her what she wanted. Then she turned around and it was Suzanne in her rose-pattern dress. She was very pale. I was shocked because I knew she was dead.

"'What do you want?' I said to her, 'You're *dead*.' thinking that if she was caught between worlds, she would understand and move on. Next I thought, "What can I do for you?" She and I were so close, we often communicated without words and I think she understood me. She reached out her hand for me. I reached towards her. And she disappeared. I felt so sad because I knew she wanted me to do something."

Angela discussed the apparition with her mother. "She's just not able to move on," her mother said. "You need to pray for her. She didn't know how to ask you."

The next day Angela went to church and lit a candle for Suzanne's soul and asked God to help her move on into Heaven.

"I wanted to push her on," says Angela, "I felt a sense of relief for her as soon as I prayed. I know she made it there." And Angela has never seen Susanne's spirit again.

THE CAN-DO SPIRIT:
Helpful ghosts

*Perhaps there walks a spirit
close by, who pities me.*
-Harry Kemp-

A surprising number of people talk about helpful things ghosts have done for them: water the plants, alert them to intruders, or just hang around. "My ghost is company for me," they tell me. "No, I wouldn't want to get rid of her." Some ghosts, it seems, need to be needed so much that they make themselves a welcome addition to the household.

THE GHOSTLY GOVERNESS

Behind the Dayton Art Institute at Superior and Grafton Avenue is a majestic Victorian home with an enclosed verandah and carriage house. It was home to Mary*, her renter, Sarah*, Sarah's children, and a ghostly governess.

It was a spring day in 1979; Sarah had just moved in. She and Mary, who both worked at the same theatre, left work at the same time but drove home by different routes. Sarah hit all the lights perfectly and sailed home quicker than usual. So she was surprised to see Mary already looking out the front bay window. She was even more surprised to find the door still locked and the burglar alarm still armed. Sarah's greeting to Mary fell into dead air.

Sarah disarmed the alarm and went on talking to Mary as she hung up her coat and put her things away. Mary still did not answer. Sarah went through the french doors into the living room. There was nobody there.

Sarah frowned, puzzled by this unsociable behavior, but she knew that Mary was having some personal problems. Besides, Mary had invited Sarah and her children to share the house with her, so Sarah tried to respect Mary's privacy. "Maybe Mary went upstairs to be alone," Sarah thought. "I won't disturb her."

She got a soda and went out to the verandah with the evening paper. As she sat there she heard the unmistakable sound of Mary's volkswagon coming up the drive and the slam of the screen door. Then Mary called, "What do you want to do for supper?" and joined Sarah on the verandah.

Sarah stared as she realized what had happened. "You won't believe this!" she said to Mary. "Before you drove up I just saw your double in the living room."

Mary smiled. "I've been wondering when my invisible house guest was going to show herself to you," Mary told Sarah. "The ghost is a dead-ringer for me except that her hair is much longer and she wears it pulled back."

Of course, when Sarah thought about it, "Mary's" clothing hadn't been right—the ghost wore a long-sleeve white blouse and a black skirt.

"The ghost is quite famous," said Mary, "she's even been seen at parties held here. And she loves children. I can tell she's much happier since you and your kids moved in."

Mary told Sarah how she had lived in an atmosphere of tension and frustration. Lights would flicker. Small articles would disappear. Mary noticed an instantaneous change in the atmosphere when Sarah and her kids moved in: the children were truly the ghostly governess's reason for living.

Sarah swears that the ghost watched over her boys who constantly talked about "the lady." She looked so much like Mary that the boys often told of things that Mary had not done, like, "Mary looked into our bedroom when she got home last night."

Sarah says that the ghost spoke to her just once. Appearing at the top of the attic stairs, the ghost told Sarah that her name was Jane and that she had been a governess in life. She showed Sarah the attic room that had been hers. And she told Sarah that she was happy that there were once again children in the house. That maternal spirit just doesn't die.

MATCH-MAKER, MATCH-MAKER....

I hear many stories of people taking "spirit" communications as absolute truth. Personally I take these stories with a big grain of salt. Not so, the unfortunate woman in this story from 1855, made a fool of by "helpful" spirits.

Mrs. Loomis* was married to a man who went off to California to seek his fortune in the gold fields. The rough-and-tumble mining camps were no place for a lady, so she was left behind in Ohio to crochet, knit warm socks, and wait for her husband to make his million. The mail service from California was not always reliable and, it must be admitted, he wasn't faithful about writing.

Mrs. Loomis, bored with her solitary life and her knitting needles, began to attend seances at a local "spirit circle." There she met Mr. Stevenson, an attractive bachelor, who soon professed to her sentiments warmer and stronger than those of ordinary friendship. Her head was in a whirl! What should she do? She hadn't heard from her husband in over three months. For all she knew, he could have fallen down a mine shaft, or been eaten by a wild buffalo, or been shot dead in some saloon.

Mrs. Loomis dabbed carefully at her eyes with her little lace handkerchief. She was so alone, so unprotected...

Mr. Stevenson patted her hand in an entirely gentlemanlike manner and suggested an eminently sensible solution: Why not ask the spirits for advice?

At the very next seance, White Eagle, a popular spirit guide, announced that a man's spirit wanted to speak to Mrs. Loomis. With tender expressions of affection, the spirit of Mr. Loomis broke the news to his wife that he was no longer in the body but was now a happy inhabitant of the "spirit land."

In fact, there was only one thing lacking that would make his happiness complete and that was to see her immediately married to Mr. Stevenson. The ceremony, he insisted, *must* be performed the very next evening in a darkened room. Mr. Loomis himself would give his blessing to the happy couple. The spirit of Mr. Loomis faded away and the medium sat up, blinked, and said innocently, "Did anything come through?"

As far as Mrs. Loomis was concerned, the voice of Heaven had spoken and must be obeyed. Her mourning for her dead husband would be cut shorter than the usual year and a day, but what did social conventions matter? She *must* honor the wishes of her late husband. So she and Mr. Stevenson were married.

Several weeks later a letter arrived from Mr. Loomis in California. The new Mrs. Stevenson paled when she saw the envelope, believing it had been sent before her dear late husband had passed over. Opening it, however, she first began to scream, then fainted. It had been written a few days *after* the seance where the "spirit" of Loomis had told of his demise and made his wishes known.

The hapless new bride confronted the medium and was told that the spirits were blameless: "So strong was the sympathy of the spirits for human woe, that they were willing to become reckless liars for its relief." It is not recorded what happened to Mr. Stevenson.[1]

PAPA G.

Alison H. lives in a late Victorian-era house in Euclid's historic district.

"When I first came into this house, I felt I belonged here. We were here for our wedding rehearsal dinner and weren't even looking for a house, but I said to my husband, 'Something wants me to be here.'

"Years later, the house went up for sale while my brother and sister-in-law were renting it. We heard stories about weird noises, things disappearing, and a ghostly man walking around the house. It stood in a former vineyard and had been owned by Papa G., who had a private wine room in the cellar during Prohibition. The owner, who was renting it to my brother and sister-in-law, was literally letting the house fall down. We like woodworking projects so we decided to buy and restore the old house.

"It was a nightmare! We replaced eight windows, two floors, two ceilings, a couple of walls, all the wiring, and some of the plumbing. I always felt someone watching over me when my husband wasn't there. It made me feel good—like someone was watching and approving.

"One day, as we were working on the house, my husband went into the storage space under the eaves and discovered five generations of *stuff*: Old TVs, 1930s magazines, all kinds of interesting junk. There was linoleum on the floor, so we assumed there was a wooden floor beneath. My husband walked back and forth, handing boxes to me. He picked up a very heavy portable TV and had just turned around when the lathe of the floor disintegrated.

"The next floor down was a good twelve to fifteen feet. There was nothing to support or catch him and had he landed with the TV on top of him, he could have been killed. I couldn't reach him, but as he was falling, something pushed him so instead of falling directly down, the TV flew out of his arms, and he flew sideways and caught his leg on a beam that was nowhere near where he was falling. This wasn't physically possible. I was in hysterics.

"'Somebody just pushed me!' he exclaimed. 'Somebody saved me!'

"Up to that moment my husband hadn't believed in ghosts. Now he looked up and said, 'Thank you, Papa G.'

"A little later, Papa G's great-grandson visited. We were describing the ghost in the house, which my son had seen. The grandson pulled out a photo.

"'That's him!' I said.

"My husband has heard and felt the ghost—particularly in the wine room in the basement and my son has also seen Papa G. there. Apparently Papa G. does not haunt alone.

"There is a lady who also haunts the property. We hear pots and pans clattering and cooking smells really early in the morning from the kitchen. Sometimes you can hear the woman humming to herself out in the kitchen or smell her lavender perfume. She appears to be from before the era of the house, but other houses previously stood on this property as well as a blacksmith's house and forge, and a tollhouse. I think she's a holdover from an earlier house. One day I had terrible writer's block and I smashed my hands down on the keyboard in frustration and crashed the computer. I was so upset I burst into tears. Suddenly, I felt a gentle hand clasping my shoulder as if to comfort me. It was so real, I reached up to pat the hand. There was no one there. But my writer's block was gone!" Someone had truly lent a helping hand.

THE PHANTOM DISHWASHER

A force that smashes dishes is a typical poltergeist manifestation. But Barbara and Shirley found one that *washed* the dishes. During the summer of 1948, Barbara spent a month with her friend Shirley at her father-in-law's summer home at Ashtabula near Lake Erie. They spent most of their time reading, eating, gossiping, napping, and walking in the park near the lake. Household chores were a low priority.

One evening, when almost every dish in the house was dirty, the women decided it was time to clean up. But the evening slipped by as they drank endless glasses of iced tea and talked until midnight. The dishes were still undone when they decided to go to bed.

"I'm too tired to do them tonight," Shirley said, "Let's leave them until morning."

Barbara agreed and they began their nightly ritual of locking the doors, making sure the window screens were hooked, and closing the downstairs windows before they went upstairs to sleep in adjoining rooms.

Barbara didn't fall asleep right away and after a bit she heard someone walking down in the kitchen. She heard water running and dishes clattering.

"Shirley must have decided to do the dishes after all," thought Barbara. "I really should help her, but I'm too tired." She drifted off to sleep.

The next morning the women got up, opened the windows, and unlocked the doors. It wasn't until breakfast that the dishes were mentioned.

Shirley said, "Gee, Babs, it was nice of you to do the dishes last night. I heard you downstairs, washing them and I meant to get up and help but I was just too tired."

Thinking she was joking, Barbara laughed. Then she realized Barbara was serious. Barbara had also heard kitchen sounds and had assumed Shirley was the kind soul catching up on the chores. They stared at each other. Both women, alone in the house, had heard someone moving about in the kitchen. The doors were locked, the windows were closed—when they went to bed and when they got up—and yet the dishes had been washed, dried, and neatly stacked by the sink all before the first light of dawn.[2]

NIGHT ROUNDS

Joy works the evening shift at a Dayton-area hospital once staffed by a religious order. She's in the Old North Building, scheduled for demolition soon. While she and her co-workers are the only living souls on their floor, they notice signs of ghostly supervision that keeps them on their toes.

"I've had times when I'm sitting at my computer and I'll get a feeling of someone standing at my door. Sometimes we get visitors looking for the way back to the main hospital so I'll look up, expecting to see someone who needs directions and there'll either be a shadow—or no one there except a very real presence.

"I've had a shadow come back and stand behind me while I was talking on the phone to a client. The first time I thought it was my co-worker coming back from her break. Sometimes we smell cigarette smoke or a pipe. Of course smoking isn't allowed in the hospital, so we search for anyone who might be smoking in the stairwells. I sometimes go sniffing around the halls, but I never find anything.

"One of things we notice, almost on a nightly basis, is the elevators going up and down. They stop at floors; the door opens long enough for a person to get or or off, but there's nobody on them. It's as if somebody's making rounds. It's gotten to be a joke, it's so predictable. After midnight it slows down. From 11 to 7 a.m., after all the real doctors have finished their rounds, it's pretty quiet.

"We've asked Housekeeping and Security about the elevators, but they don't know anything about it. Security guards make their rounds, but you know when the guards are coming down the hall—because they're *there*. Our floor was formerly a patient care area. A lot of the doctors actually use this elevator during the day, but someone's using it at night!

"Once my friend Jackie took a break and while she was waiting for the elevator, it stopped at our floor without her calling for it. The door opened. She told me, 'I knew someone was getting off, so I just stepped back and said, "Hello, Doctor?"'

"On Memorial Day in 1997 I watched several shadows crossing and recrossing the halls between rooms. I've never seen it that active! I could sense that one was a stocky lady— very efficient, very no-nonsense—someone who definitely knew what she was doing, checking her patients. I just told myself, 'That's OK. I've seen shadows before.'

When Joy told Jackie about the multiple shadows, Jackie said, "Don't they know it's a holiday?"

"Nuns and doctors don't have holidays," Joy replied. "And they probably all were out earlier at picnics!"

"A little later, that same day, as I was talking to someone on the phone, I heard footsteps coming down the hall. They stopped right at our door. That was it. I shut the door. I sensed brown leather loafers. This felt more like a doctor, but there was no shadow with this one."

"The main chapel is on our floor; there's *lots* of presence in there at night. Some people have walked down there, looking for a quiet spot to sit. They come back after a few minutes. I don't know what's there, but it's so *full*. I tried to go in once; that lasted about two minutes. No, we don't go in *there* at night.

Joy finds the whole thing a little unnerving, "But there's no question that they're benevolent. Even that time the shadow came and stood behind me, I felt it was listening, monitoring. Was I being kind to the person? Once satisfied that we were doing our job, it went away. They want us to know that they care.

"For many nuns, this was their whole focus. They lived strict lives, dedicating their being to taking care of others. They're still dedicated to it."

MISTRESS SUZANNE

She was called "the ugliest woman in Painesville." But Mistress Suzanne had more substantial charms, namely a large fortune, that attracted Joseph Rider, the founder of what is now known as Rider's 1812 Inn. He was in financial trouble. She was his third wife. Just six weeks after their marriage in 1834, the newspapers reported her death under "strange and mysterious circumstances."

Rider must have been the kind to marry in haste. Only six weeks after Suzanne's death, he married wife number four who gave birth to twins six months after the wedding.

"I call that 'pioneer divorce'," innkeeper Elaine Crane commented dryly. "You figure it out." Elaine, owner of Rider's 1812 Inn, is a delightfully chatty lady, who obviously loves people and innkeeping. She is also a wonderful storyteller, and tells some fascinating tales about the ghostly Suzanne, who still roams the Inn.

When we were first doing construction and all the windows and doors were off, there were incidents. At the time I blamed the local children for coming in and taking keys and tools. I was complaining to everybody. "Oh, don't worry about the kids," the neighbors said "they're afraid of the ghost."

Everything was fine for about three weeks. Then, in the middle of the night, I heard somebody calling my name. I went out and saw a candle lit in the hallway. We are carefully to always blow candles out before we go to bed because this is an old timber building. I got upset with my partner, because he went to bed after me and I thought he had left it burning. I blew it out, and as I bent over, I could see *another* lit candle in the next room. There were about five candles in five different rooms and they led me to the dining room where the big Bunn coffee maker was on. The coffee had boiled down to nothing and the pot was sparking. I turned it off and stuck the pot in water. Then I looked around. The candles I had been following from room to room were extinguished—even the ones I hadn't blown out. I thought "How strange!"

Several weeks later, we had a guest who is a retired fire chief from New York staying at the inn. He was really into the Inn and its stories. As we were sitting up late, I told him about the strange night with the candles. "In our experience, that's always a good sign that the building likes you," he told me, which I thought was weird. Then he added, "The real test will be, if you are in tune with the building, you will know when there is danger." I thought this was even stranger.

That night, I woke up with a start. I was expecting strange things by now. I went down the hall and heard a tapping coming from the basement. I was lifting the latch to go into the basement, which is an old-fashioned root-cellar with our mechanical equipment crammed in, when I realized that Dick, the firechief, was there.

"The building called to me," he said, "There is a problem in the basement and we have to fix it."

We found that the bottom had fallen off the hot water heater. Gallons of scalding water were flooding the basement and were within inches of our computers. Dick waded through the water, burning himself in the process, and turned off the water at the main. We worked for three and a half hours pumping out water and protecting the heating, computer, and phone equipment. That was the third incident.

When the very first incident happened, I didn't realize its significance. This took place the August before we opened. One wall in the inn was set with antique tile imported from Italy. I wanted to use it in my bathroom. The tileworker didn't want to chip it off because the tiles were so fragile. It was very fussy work, trying to move the tiles without breaking any.

One Sunday, I was home alone, with no paperwork and no closets to clean and I thought, "This is the time for the tile." So I drove to the inn. It was a sunny day, the lawnmowers were buzzing, and it was hot, so I was wearing a tank top, sandals and cut-offs. The radio was blaring a baseball game. I started chipping away.

Well, I hit too hard, knocked something loose and the entire wall came down on me. The broken tile was razor-sharp and laid me open from breast to waist. I could feel the blood running down my leg, warm and sticky. I was pinned by the weight of the wall and could not get up. I was gasping and yelling, but no one could hear me outside over the lawnmowers. I was really frightened. I knew tile was sticking in me and the pain was beginning to spread.

We had a cat named Sasha. I saw her in the next room and I felt like she was watching me, concerned. I was dizzy and feeling faint. Then I felt something brush behind my hair, which I assumed was the cat. Then the wall lifted enough for me to free my right hand, and to push the tile away. Covered with blood, I drove myself to the hospital where I had sixteen stitches.

I called my husband to pick me up; they wouldn't let me drive home, I had lost so much blood. Well, I'm an innkeeper, so no matter what, I had to go back and lock the door. My husband didn't like it, but I told him, "There's blood all over the floor, it will stain; we've got to go back." So we went and there was blood all over the place and we cleaned it up. I was telling him how the cat had brushed against me. My husband looked at the floor. "What do you mean?" he said, "There was no cat in here." I looked down; my husband looked down. In the dust that had settled on the floor, there were no cat footprints, only the prints of my sandals—and the marks of a pair of high-heeled shoes.

So we told each other that somebody got in while I was in the hospital, but there were no footprints anywhere else and nothing had been taken. After the previous two incidents, I thought back and that one began to have a different significance....

One of our guests at the inn, a physicist named Larry, always pooh-poohed our assertion that the ghost opened the front door when the building was in danger. This door locks on both sides with a key, but it still opens and a breeze comes in and warns us. One night there was a double-feature James Bond on TV. Larry wanted to sit up and watch it, so I said, "Larry, you close down. Just turn off the coffee pot before you go to bed."

The next morning there was a half-inch of snow in the dining room from the open door. Of course he'd forgotten to turn the coffee pot off and *she* had to open the door to cool it down. Larry took the day off from work and spent it measuring things. He couldn't explain it. The next time he came to visit, I found him sitting at the bar, telling a Suzanne story. We converted him!

My family sleeps in the back quarters, away from the main part of the Inn; this provides privacy for both us and our guests. One night I was awakened by a call from the Painesville Police Department: "Your door is standing wide open. Are you OK?" I was a municipal court judge and I was very tough on domestic violence. There are a few men out there who might still want me dead, so the police keep a friendly eye on me.

"I'm fine," I said.

"Just come out, so we can see you're OK," the officer said, which is standard operating procedure. As I got to the window, after pulling up my jeans, I saw the police car pulling out of the driveway. I phoned the dispatcher and jokingly said, "Joyce, where's Painesville's Finest?"

"Oh, they didn't mean to embarrass you. When they saw you in the second floor hall in your nightgown and you waved, they didn't want to make you get dressed."

The police described the person they saw to Joyce, and it wasn't me. I'm short with long brown hair and I look a little like Ali McGraw. The woman they saw was tall, thin, plain and blond. All the guests were in their rooms with the doors locked....

When Dan Quayle was in town, the inn was used as Republican headquarters. There were people all over and we worked throughout the night. We were exhausted! The headquarters pulled out by Sunday morning and we had only one bridal couple coming that night. That afternoon, I got a call from the best man. Due to a flight time change, the couple needed to cancel their reservation. Normally we have a 48-hour cancellation policy, but I'd had that kind of problem myself. I was actually kind of grateful because I didn't need to wait up until midnight and get up the next morning to fix them breakfast.

At 9 p.m. Sunday, we battened everything down at the inn and I went back home. At eight the next morning the building manager called me there. "Mrs. Crane, who's in room 6? The light's on!"

"Nobody's in the Bridal Suite," I said. And I came flying over to see what was going on.

I knocked on the door and said, "Excuse me, who are you?"

"We're the bridal couple," they said. "we had reservations."

"And you're one of the rudest people we've ever met," the bride continued, irritably, "I know we got in late last night. I know you were in your nightgown. But when we asked for Coke, you never even turned any lights on, just pointed upstairs."

"I let you in last night?" I said. I had no recollection of it. I thought, 'I must have been more tired than I realized...' And I apologized as best I could. I went home and took a nap. When I woke up, I remembered that I had left the inn the night before with the head server and the bartender, leaving the Inn securely locked up. It turned out the best man had played a prank. He actually admitted to me he had cancelled the room, hoping to leave the newlyweds with no reservations. I never told the couple....

I consider Suzanne one of my staff but the most unreliable one. I can't count on her! Suzanne was an innkeeper and her premature death cut short her career. Once we articulated that, all those things that could have been explained other ways fell into place. What we didn't expect was the marvelous reaction of customers and guests. People are comfortable with her. There are 852 drawers in this place; there's an enormous attic. Keys and other things get lost. I've seen members of the staff put their hands on their hips and say, "Suzanne, we've got to have it now." And I admit, I'll ask, "C'mon, Suzanne, help us!"

I want to emphasize that the Inn is *not* spooky. People say they never feel alone; that it feels cozy, warm, friendly; that they've never had such a good night's sleep. It's almost as if somebody extra is taking care of you. I sometimes wait up by myself until three in the morning for a guest who failed to cancel, but I'm never uncomfortable.

We've got Mistress Suzanne's Dining Room and Master's Joseph's pub, and a sitting room in between because they didn't like each other. Every six to eight weeks, when we're telling a story, the cash register flies open or we hear knocking on the sealed door. I give tours to the Boy and Girl Scouts for their history badges. We finish off with an Ice Cream Social or a High Tea. We take pictures and sometimes there is an extra shadowy figure in the photos.

Perhaps Mistress Suzanne is there, too, listening to the stories.

5

GHOSTS THAT WOULD CRACK A MIRROR: Ugly apparitions and hostile hauntings

Whose horrid image doth unfix my hair
And make my seated heart knock at my ribs?
-William Shakespeare-

Sometimes we think of ghosts as lovely, transparent women in filmy white draperies. Ghosts of relatives often appear as their old familiar selves, homely and loved. But not all ghosts are attractive, familiar, or loved. Some ghosts just don't fall into any category except terrifying....

THE UGLY UNCONSCIOUS

In 1959, Mary P. was lying awake in a house off Fudge Rd. near the High School in Beavercreek, pondering a choice. She and her husband had fallen in love with a beautiful farm in Eaton. It was their dream property. Yet Mary was troubled about whether or not they should move. On one hand, their daughter and her family would soon be moving back to Beavercreek from Texas and Mary wanted to be close by to enjoy her grandchildren. On the other hand, most of her family lived in Eaton. And it was a *very* beautiful farm.

Eventually Mary drifted off to sleep. She woke to a voice calling her name insistently: "Mary...Mary...*Mary*!" Sleepily she opened her eyes. Then they snapped open.

At the foot of her bed she saw half of a shrouded shape floating in the air. She could make out a mouth and eyes, but the rest of the face was a nightmarish foggy blur, like a sodden cotton ball.

Mary sat up, somehow unafraid. The lips did not move, but the thing spoke in a strange voice—neither male nor female, saying firmly,

"Under no circumstances are you to move to Eaton, Ohio." And the hideous apparition faded away.

Mary never told her husband. He had been raised in a haunted house in Tennessee and he would have insisted on moving out of the Beavercreek house immediately. Somehow Mary and her husband decided against moving to Eaton. It proved to be the right decision.

Mary's husband died shortly after her vision. Her daughter and family, newly arrived from Texas, proved to need her help. The apparition could have been her subconscious, just trying to be helpful. Mary wonders about one thing, though. If it was just her subconscious—why did it have to be so ugly?

A HOMELESS HAUNT

The police officer was tall and dark with a handsome mustache. I had noticed him standing in the dark in the back of the lecture hall as I gave my talk to a group of students at the University of Dayton. After the students had finished their breathless recitals of accurate predictions by ouija boards and mysterious disappearances of leftover pizza, the officer approached. He seemed like a man who had seen it all and privately despised it.

"You know Liberty Hall?" he said without introduction.

I nodded. I had read some stories about the building in the paper. "Do you want to walk through it?"

"Now?" It was after 9:00 p.m.

He nodded. "I won't go in there after dark. But I'd go with *you*,"

"Thanks," I said, making a face, but I went. As we walked the University of Dayton campus towards the Hall, he told me about fellow security officers who refused to patrol the building after dark. I had already warned him not to give me any specifics and he didn't. The building was a warm red brick, a smallish, rectangular building, two stories high, the oldest original building on the university campus. I looked up at the windows but nothing looked back.

There were plenty of lights on inside as Officer J. unlocked the door and I had to say the building didn't look particularly sinister. We started in the basement. Liberty Hall's many offices were arranged in an outer circle around an inner core of more offices. All of the hallways were brightly lit. Some doors opened into darkened offices. I felt nothing in the basement; nothing on the first floor; nothing on the second floor —until I turned the last corner.

Standing unsteadily in the hall was a ghostly man. He was a shattered hulk, bent to one side, like a hunchback. He had a long, shaggy beard and mustache. Around his mouth, the hair was stained yellowish-brown with nicotine. He was dressed in many layers of ragged clothing and as he walked, he dragged one foot, painfully heaving it forward with each step. The worst thing about the apparition was—he dribbled. A string of saliva hung, glistening, from his broken-toothed mouth.

The hallway was too narrow for me to go forward without walking right through him. "I think I'll just go back *this* way," I said brightly. I circled back around to where the officer was standing and stepped into a well-lit corner office. There, I was safe.

Outside Liberty Hall Officer J. lit up a cigarette and two of his companions joined him to hear what I would say and to tell their stories. I got the feeling that the old man was mostly confined to limping up and down that particular stretch of hall, but officers also reported seeing him looking out of the windows or seeing his silhouette in the darkened offices.

Others have had experiences elsewhere in the building. A young couple was waiting in the foreign students' lounge on the second floor. It was 3:30 a.m. when they heard someone walk from the rear of the building downstairs to the front door.

They had their backs to the door, but were curious about who else was in the building so late at night. They went to the head of the stairs to investigate.

As they peered around the corner, looking down the stairs, they heard a person climbing towards them. The invisible climber passed *between* them, and continued down the hall. They looked at each other and then dashed down the stairs and out of the building.[1]

Who could the old man have been? A long-retired University of Dayton professor told me the following story:

Liberty Hall was at one time an infirmary for students and for some university workmen who had rooms there. One morning in the early hours, one of the workmen in a back room on the first floor was suddenly awakened from a deep sleep. He looked around the room to see what had woken him. Suddenly he noticed next to his bed an old man in somber dress with an abundant gray beard steadily staring at him. The worker was about to ask his uninvited visitor what he wanted at such an hour. Even as he looked at the old man, waiting for an explanation, the figure slowly dissolved into thin air and never bothered him again.

Having shared his experience with some of the faculty later in the day, the worker was told that old, disabled workers had been housed there and some had died in that room.

Could the man that I saw be one of these workers? Or was he some homeless tramp taken in by the Marianist Brothers, only to die in their infirmary? Whoever he is, on your next visit to the University of Dayton, slip next door to the Immaculate Conception Chapel and say a prayer for the repose of his poor limping soul.

BURNT GHOST

"One of my most frightening experiences didn't happen to me directly," Candi told me, "When I was in high school a guy named Ray* moved into town. He lived a short distance down Rt. 117 near Spencerville, with his mother and grandmother. Ray was a big, easy-going guy. He played football. Making up imaginative stories wasn't exactly his strong point. In fact, we became close friends because I'm fairly good at writing and I helped him with a lot of his papers.

"Ray and I usually talked on the phone when we got home from school. One day, we were having our usual after school conversation when Ray suddenly got very quiet. He asked me to hold on a second and put down the phone. A minute or two later, the phone went dead. I figured Ray would call back when he got done with whatever he was doing and started on my homework. Ten minutes later, Ray showed up on my doorstep. He must have ridden his bike to my house at top speed because he was so winded he couldn't talk. When he calmed down, he told me he didn't think he could ever go back to his house. Then he told me why.

"While we were talking on the phone, he had heard someone come in through the front door. It was too early for anyone in his family to be home, so he had asked me to wait while he went downstairs to investigate. But as he reached for the doorknob, an overwhelming feeling of fear made him step back. Through his closed door he heard someone walking up the stairs. Whoever it was stopped outside his door. He saw the doorknob turning as if someone was trying come into his room. Since his door was locked, the person walked to the next door—his grandmother's room—and he heard the door open and shut. He didn't think it was a ghost at first—why would a locked door stop a ghost? He changed his mind after thoroughly searching the house and finding no one. That's when he ran for it.

"Ray asked his grandmother about the experience. She was evasive about the strange things she'd experienced, but she did tell Ray that a woman had died in the house a few years before she had moved in. The story was that the woman had been raking and burning leaves when a spark landed on her clothes and set her ablaze.

No one had liked this woman very much because of her sour disposition, so she didn't have many visitors. Eventually a woman from church stopped by. The visitor noticed that the

car was in the driveway, but nobody came to the door when she
knocked. She walked around to knock at the back door. That's
when she found the old woman's charred remains.

"Just last year, a guy I was going out with drove me home
and on the way we passed by that old house. He's not from
this area and he knew nothing about its grim story. As we
drove by, he checked the rear-view mirror and nearly wrecked
the car. In a panic, he pulled over, jumped out, and circled the
car, wildly searching for something. When he came back, he
explained that he had seen a black, bloated face in the mirror
that seemed to be chasing the car."

THE DARK SIDE OF THE HOUSE

When she was 14, Alison moved into a stately old home
that had been one of the original houses on the Cleveland
Heights street. It was (and still is) a large, airy, side-by-side
duplex with original dark wood trim and wood-burning
fireplaces. The two sides, consisting of three full floors plus
attic and basement, are mirror-images of each other, yet one
reflects light, the other only darkness...

"I knew from the first moment I saw it that there was
something odd about the other side of the house. My Mom and
I are "sensitive" and Mom had always said, 'We can't live on
that side of the house.' There was something cold, something
unwelcoming about it, while the side we lived in was the exact
opposite."

Alison lived in the left-hand side of the house as she was
growing up and never had any problems there. When she
married for the first time, and had a child, the right side of the
duplex fell vacant and her mother suggested that the new
family move in.

"We had just lost our apartment lease very suddenly and
we had nowhere we could move in a hurry. I convinced myself
that it wouldn't be so bad and it *would* be better than being out
on the street..."

Alison felt immediately that their side of the house was not
particularly friendly. Even in warm weather, "columns of cold

air" stood in parts of the dining room and kitchen, raising goose-bumps on those who walked through them. The basement's "aura" was particularly hostile.

"I found that the hairs on the back of my neck would rise every time I hit the bottom of the steps. I took to sorting and folding all of my laundry upstairs in the kitchen, so as to spend as short a time as possible downstairs. I always felt two or three people staring at me. I could not take my infant son down there—he would start shrieking the minute we passed through the basement door and could not be consoled until we safely reached the kitchen again."

Alison had a home office on the third floor. "It was brightly lit and cheerful. Or should have been." One inside wall was always icy to the touch, even in the heat of summer. And Alison's son refused to use the playpen set up in the office for him, even though he played happily in his playpen downstairs.

"That, coupled with the fact that I always felt like I was being watched in this room, caused me to do most of my work while he napped and *never* after dark. I simply couldn't bring myself to enter that room at night."

One office wall held a bookshelf filled with oversized art books. It was some six feet away from the playpen. One afternoon, Alison heard a loud series of crashes up in her office. Racing upstairs, she found that every one of those heavy art books was neatly stacked in her son's empty playpen.

"They weren't lying helter-skelter as they would be if they had fallen. And the shelves were still intact. I was extremely spooked. I don't believe I went back into that upstairs room alone again, willingly. I made my husband clear my stuff out of there! Even on sunny days, there was a horrible icy feeling in that room. The whole side of that house was angry."

Alison and her husband slept in the master bedroom, directly below the third-floor guest bedroom. "It was a bright, airy room, with none of the ill feelings of the office. One night, around 2:30 in the morning, my husband and I were jerked awake by the sounds of horrible crashing—furniture being scraped across the wooden floor above our heads, splintering wood, and breaking glass. We looked at each other and my husband said, 'I'm not going to go check. Are *you* going to check?' We were terrified, but both of us decided it would be the better part of valor to wait until daylight to investigate. Frankly, we were both too scared to go up and find out what was going on."

"Finally morning came and we went upstairs to check. The room was bright with morning light and everything was as it should be. This was probably our most frightening experience. Nothing had been moved. No explanation was ever forthcoming, but I can tell you it was quite some time before either of us slept soundly again. From that point on, I shunned the third floor unless absolutely necessary."

Alison and her husband eventually divorced and they both moved out of the house. It was then that Alison learned some of the truth about her side of the duplex.

"When my parents first bought the house, they began renting out the other side of it to groups of students or to apprentices and actors from the Cleveland Playhouse. Apparently, there was a fairly brisk turnover of tenants who occupied that office room. No one would give solid reasons except to say they were uncomfortable there. After all of my troubles, I hunted down some people who had lived in that room. They didn't want to talk at first. Nobody wants anybody to think they're crazy. But after I told them, 'I had some really hideous experiences in there.' they began to open up.

One young man used to see an old man standing there, staring at him from the closet door. "He could just *feel* the malice. The ghost never actually did anything, but his look was enough to curl the guy's hair. One woman told me something that made *my* hair stand on end. Had I known of it before moving in, I think I might have turned my mother down when she offered the place to us."

What she heard was this: One night 'Linda' was in her single bed in the office room. Normally she didn't sleep well in the room, but she was sick and drifted off to sleep quickly.

She awakened with a start to feel someone climb into bed with her and lay their hand on her leg. Thinking that one of her roommates was playing a joke on her, she reached up quickly and turned on her bedside light. There was no one there. Suddenly, she felt like the room was freezing. Out of the corner of her eye, right next to the cold wall of the closet, she saw an old man, standing with his hands clasped in front of him, glaring angrily at her. She turned to face him, and he vanished into the open door of the closet. She moved out very soon after that."

Alison has discovered a little of the history of the house. "When it was first built, a mother and father lived on one side; their son and his wife lived on the other. I suspect that the mother and father lived on the cold side, but that is sheer conjecture."

Did she do any research to find out why that side of the house felt so bad? "I thought I'd just leave sleeping ghosts lie," Alison commented ruefully. "I didn't really want to know."

THE PLAYTOWNE* CURSE

Anne Oscard and I were running late and we weren't quite sure where we were going. I drove while she squinted at the addresses. Although it was the only large building with a parking lot in the mainly residential area, we nearly drove past it. I saw a woman standing by a high fence to the side of the building.

"Ah," I thought. "She's waiting for us." I parked the car and we walked over to where I'd seen her—a matter of less than a minute—but there was no one there. The fence was too high to climb and I couldn't see a gate. No, I thought, she couldn't be....

Then a whole section of fence swung outward and the woman I'd seen before stepped forward. Her name was June*, a teacher at the Playtowne* Daycare Center. She and several other staff members had been impressed by Anne's tarot-card readings and had asked us to come visit.

Right away I noticed a smell—mould, I thought. My heart began to beat irregularly as soon as I stepped onto the linoleum from the carpet. I had a strange reluctance to step off the carpet anywhere. June introduced us to three more of the staff. Sylvia*, Kathy* and Liz* were in a state. On one hand, they knew something wasn't right at the center; yet they were terrified that we would discover something and they would lose their jobs for blowing the whistle. Anne and I tried to assure them that they would be completely anonymous.

The center was basically one big room, with separate spaces for kitchen, bathrooms, and an office, partitioned off with shelving and screens. Although the cement block walls were decorated with bright-colored posters and crayoned artwork, it was a grim place. Even the lights looked dingy. Anne and I wandered around separately, muttering to ourselves and taking notes.

I looked down the short hall and was instantly afraid of something I couldn't see. There were two bathrooms—one for the children at the end of the hall; one for the staff next to it. The staff bath was fine; the human skeleton poster next to it added an appropriately macabre touch. But I was reluctant to enter the children's bathroom—it made me dizzy. I shut the door firmly, trying to shut whatever it was inside.

I hesitated outside the kitchen. I could see over the counter into the room; the far corner was unnaturally dark. Something hovered near the ceiling. It wasn't friendly. I stepped into the kitchen and began trembling so much that I had to sit down. I tottered over to the teachers' office area and sank into a desk chair. For what seemed like a half hour I sat there, sunk in weakness and despair. I felt paralyzed—as if I'd had a stroke and couldn't move. At last I was able to pry myself out of the chair. I went to stand on the opposite side of the room and we began to talk.

"I feel water under this building," Anne said. "It's almost as though the whole building is floating on an underground lake." She swayed back and forth to illustrate. "Is there water in this area?"

June said there are artesian springs all over the neighborhood. "I know because I've lived here all my life and my sister lives a few streets over.

"In fact," she added "after we had the parking lot repaved, this green slime with an awful odor oozed through the blacktop and cracked it."

There was also a cold spot in the hall and a bathroom drain that a plumber said was non-functional but which always had water in it.

Sylvia, the cook, was also the janitor. One evening as she was working she saw an old woman in a housedress and apron at the sink. "Her facial expression was like, 'Get the hell out!' Sylvia recalled. Another worker had seen a woman in the hall. Anne felt the presence of a pipe smoker who could have been male or female; she also sensed the name "Agatha."

Everyone we interviewed said that they were sick all year, not unusual in a daycare, but got better when they were away from the building during summer vacation. Their ailments were not the typical colds and sore throats, but lung and skin problems, adult acne, that also healed during breaks. Various staff members heard doors opening when they were alone. Things disappeared almost daily: a plastic toy pizza, books and tapes.

"Surely that's not unusual with so many kids?" I asked.

"No, but these toys weren't even put out yet. They were still in the teachers' cabinets."

Anne climbed up the fold-down staircase to the attic. Almost immediately she came groping her way back down. She had been stricken with a blinding headache. I've been on many ghost-hunts with Anne; I've never seen her so affected by a site. She suspected formaldehyde. She had similar reactions in college when dissecting specimens stored in the liquid. Only formaldehyde leeches out of insulation within a month or two. The building was much older than that.

During the 1940s, Wright Field in Dayton boomed. People from Kentucky and other points south flooded into the area in search of work. There wasn't enough housing, so people lived in shacks and shanties, even tents. Fifty years later the area is still known by some as "Little Kentucky." Could the pipe-smoking, aproned woman have come from this time and place?

The building stands near Wright-Patterson Air Force Base and several large factories. Is it possible that some kind of toxic waste was buried under the building, making everyone ill, possibly even causing hallucinations? Toxins like dioxin have been known to cause skin problems and illness. The ghost of a horrid old woman, mysterious illnesses, green slime oozing through blacktop—it was an ugly picture. The staff seemed devoted to the children but I was happy to hear that the center was soon to move to a new building.

As of this writing, a rarely used office is now the only occupant of the building. Or is it?

THE THING IN THE CELLAR

Louise's father was a mortician and funeral director. In 1957, he worked for a funeral home in Lebanon, Ohio. The funeral home building had been built at the same time as the early 19th century Golden Lamb Hotel.

"The place was IMMENSE, so we moved into the first floor, not using any other part of the building. Since it was such an ancient house, we heard all the moans and groans an old house usually produces. My sister and I had no other play-mates and we loved to explore the house. We found an old stable which led into an incredible room through a tunnel which, you could tell from the dust on the floor, had not been used in ages.

"I never really felt anything in the house until we went downstairs to the coal cellar. It had a stone floor, dirt walls like a root cellar and I hated the place. It even *smelled* old. Its only light came from the coal chute door. There was also a large metal door opening out to the backyard. This door was secured by a heavy cross-bar inside. Steep, rickety stairs led out of the cellar to a door on the first floor, filled with wavey, frosted glass that opened into the breakfast room.

"One afternoon I was alone in the house with our German Shepherd, Joey. He started barking and growling and I ran into the kitchen to see what was wrong. He was in the breakfast room and I saw his hair standing on end as he glared at something behind the frosted glass.

'Joey, quit making so much noise!' I scolded.

Through the glass, I saw a figure staring back at me. It seemed solid, like a real person, and had its hands cupped around its eyes, as if trying to see into the room through the glass. I couldn't make out a face, but it had long, long hair or a long veil. I couldn't tell definitely if it was a man or a woman, but I got the impression it was a man. It had hands like a man and a light-colored face. It was much taller than me, maybe between 5'6" and 5'8." It was standing on the tiny landing; I could hear it pushing on the door. The "Thing on the Wing," in *The Twilight Zone*—that's what it reminded me of.

"I backed out of the room, screaming like a banshee. I ran into the tunnel leading next door to the funeral home where my dad was working. He came running back with the owner of the building and by then, the dog had calmed down. The key was still inside the lock of the frosted door.

"We walked into the cellar to find that the metal outer door was solidly closed—and the coal dust on the floor was completely undisturbed by footprints other than our own."

6

LIONS AND TIGERS AND SCARES, OH MY!:
Strange and ghostly animals

His hand hath formed the crooked serpent.
-Job 26:13-

It is strange how often wild animals seem to escape from circuses to roam Ohio. Stranger still how often they can photographed, leave behind footprints and droppings, yet never be caught. For example, bears** and baboons**, catamans and cougars, lions and tigers, five-foot high birds and a thirteen-foot-long python.

1994 saw a spate of tiger-spottings in Montgomery and Highland Counties. In May of 1994 a tiger was reported in a field near Washington Church Road in the Dayton area. The same witness saw and videotaped the creature the following day. The video appeared to show a large cat—whether feral or just overfed, police could not say.

Dayton police took initial reports seriously. They called in experts from the Cincinnati Zoo to explain what signs to look for including tracks, animal droppings, and patches of grass pressed flat by the resting cat. No such signs were detected—even after the sighting area was baited with fresh meat.[3]

**A 30-inch baboon was found dead near Aurora in Portage County. The Dog Warden said there were no reports of a missing baboon and no circus or animal show in the area.[1] A West Jefferson man reported a 4-foot-tall bear in his backyard. The animal fled into the bushes and was not found by police.[2]*

Highland County officials also had little to go on: a 4-inch paw print with no trace of claws. Witnesses reporting something bigger than a dog chasing deer. The first report came on November 10th from a woman who saw a striped tan and white animal walking across a field. Several minutes later, another woman called in to report something big and brown chasing a deer across a field about two miles north of the first sighting. The next day, a neighbor found a deer carcass in the woods near the sighting.[4]

And while we're talking of big cats, what was a lion doing in Mentor, Ohio? On the evening of June 3, 1992, several reports came into the Mentor Police Department of a 7-foot-long creature with a mane, crouching low to the ground. "It definitely was a lion," witness David S. insisted. "He had a mane, and that thing had big shoulders on him. I was kind of scared when I saw him. I was wondering, 'How'd he get here?' That thing could eat a person." Further investigation turned up nothing substantial. The police suggested that witnesses saw a large golden retriever.[5]

This eerily echoes a report from Carthage of a ghostly man accompanied by a shaggy dog the size of a young lion. The duo was spotted for several nights at a Carthage factory in August of 1948.[6]

Where do these cat-creatures come from? Where do they go, after leaving behind strange paw-prints and dead prey? Are we humans being played with, as a cat toys with a captive mouse?

THE GREAT SERPENTS

Serpent Mound is a place of strange power. Sacred to Native Americans and more recently the site of the New Age "Harmonic Convergence" gathering in August, 1987, the immense earthworks shaped like a snake swallowing an egg have fascinated spiritual seekers for centuries.

Recently geologists have discovered gravitational and magnetic anomalies at the site. Ohio's senior state geologist Michael G. Hansen says that a cataclysmic event he calls a "cryptoexplosion" took place there: for example, a volcano, or a meteorite crash that blasted a hole in the earth's crust. No one has discovered just what event took place so long ago; it left no trace except for the magnetic and gravity anomalies.[7]

Could these anomalies have drawn Native Americans to the site just as they continue to draw hundreds of mystic seekers to this day?

Art Caruso of Youngstown has been drawn to the Great Serpent for over 30 years.

"On Oct 20, 1981, my photographer and I traveled to Adams County near Peebles, Ohio to explore and gather information on the large serpent effigy located on a hill that is now a state park. We arrived at the site at 1 p.m. and wasted no time getting to work. Larry started his photography work on the south end of the park. I went north along the body of the serpent taking compass readings and observing the surrounding area.

"At one point along the body, I suddenly had a feeling that someone was watching me and that the individual was some-where close by. The feeling was so strong that I stopped what I was working on as if someone had called me. I looked around but could not see anyone. My mind kept on sending me mental images of a man who appeared primitive and old. He looked as if he was trying to speak to me, but I could not understand him.

"After a few seconds the scene changed. I noticed other people standing around the mound. They looked just like the man near me. It all happened so quick! The next thing was real spooky—everyone disappeared and the serpent lay alone for a second, then started to shake, trembling the ground like it wanted to come alive."

On June 25-26, 1997, Art went back to the serpent with three assistants, Peggy, Sue, and Veronica. On the first fold of the serpent, not far from the head, Sue and Art were taking compass readings. Art was on one side of the serpent's body; Sue was on the other.

"The serpent's body is rather high at that point and I could only see Sue's head. We had to yell to talk to each other over the mound. She was about 15 feet away from me. All of a sudden she disappeared! I called over. She didn't answer. I walked up and down the mound, trying to see if I could see her at an angle. Nothing. Then Veronica, who was about 100 feet away, noticed what was going on. *She* could see Sue and she whistled at her."

This seemingly broke the spell and suddenly Sue was back in sight. Sue told Art that she had been there all along, not stooped down or anything. Strangely, the same thing had happened to Sue: Art had disappeared from her sight. "Sue said she couldn't figure out where *I* was or why I wasn't talking to her. That spot on the serpent was the only place we ever had trouble."

Late in the day on the 26th, Art's friend Beth* met them at the site. After a warning from Art about the power of the site, Beth and the three other women went to the Chronicle Burial Mound southeast of the serpent while Art continued his temperature readings. Beth later said she felt something overwhelming her, but she didn't quite understand what it was.

The day, which had been beautiful, suddenly clouded over. Art played me a tape recording made that day. There is a prolonged roar, like jets overhead. Common enough, but there is something else on the tape that chilled my blood. The three women said that Beth appeared to pass into a trance and began to speak.

I was not there so I cannot tell about that. However, I am familiar with mediums who claim to channel ancient languages and bygone spirits. This was different. The woman's voice was frail, pleading and terribly sad. Although I am not an expert, the words sounded like a Native American language. The voice meandered on and on in a heart-broken lament. I felt I was intruding on a private moment: a woman beseeching her loved one to return.

I don't know if Beth connected with some spirit still mourning her dead, or was merely echoing an ancient sorrow.

Art wants to play the tape for Native American linguists to see if they can identify the language. The emotion needed no translation.

Another Great Serpent was reported in 1944, but this was not an ancient earthwork. A 13-foot "python" was captured at Doylestown in 1944. Elizabeth Langguth graciously wrote me about the snake, which was discovered in her pasture:

"As I remember it, it was early evening, just after the supper hour and I was doing up the dishes in the old basement kitchen in the farmhouse. My husband and the children, ages 11, 15, and 16, were somewhere out in the yard. My husband had noticed a young man bolt out of our woods and jump in his car and roar off up the road towards town and had mildly wondered what was his big hurry. Soon after that, a car came tearing down the road, stopping right on the bend. Doors flew open and boys jumped out and scurried down the bank into the pasture. Out of curiosity, my husband and the kids went up the road to see what was going on. The boys were dragging this huge snake up the bank and laying it along the road.

My daughter hurried back to the house and insisted that I come quickly and see the biggest snake ever. I did and there he was, all 13 ft. 6 in. of him. Someone had propped a stick in his mouth to hold it open and display the teeth....

Bill Hummel had been hunting mushrooms in our woods. The snake was found on land adjoining the Clyde Meyers place, on farmland that belonged to Charles and Elizabeth Langguth. The part about the grass being trampled down for an area of 30 ft. where the snake died in its death throes is pure hog wash. No one knows how he died. It was very dead when found. The grass was trampled down by the dozen or so Doylestown kids who scrambled down the bank and ooohed and ahhed before dragging him up on the road.

The snake laid there for a couple of days. Then some youngsters came along in the dead of night and dragged it to the village of Warwick. I've been told that the village fathers insisted that it be removed, due to the odor. From here there are two versions of the story. One is that the python ended up at a gasoline [sic] station in a tub of formaldehyde in Barberton. The other is that it ended up at Campfield Hickman's mortuary in Barberton in a tub of formaldehyde. I think the former is more likely correct. Somehow, I can not imagine those two very staid and proper gentlemen who operated that establishment condoning anything of the kind...

There was much speculation around town as to where the snake came from. Some old timers were sure he had been living in an old mine shaft that ran through our property. I doubt that. If he was in fact a python, which is what every one said it was, it could hardly have survived our climate. Most people were of the opinion that it got lost from a show that might have passed through our area and simply expired from natural causes.

I've seen a photo of the mysterious python**, but I have to confess that I was disappointed. I was expecting some barrel-thick monster capable of cutting swathes the size of car tires through the meadows. Instead, the pitifully withered python was about the thickness of a walking-stick. But in the photo it is *very* long—eight men and one boy long, to be exact.

**You can see it in *Doylestown 1827-1952*, by Mrs. B.E. Sever, (Rittman Press, [1952])

HORSE HEAVEN

Louise shares her 6-acre farm in Germantown with horses, geese, turkeys, a 6-foot iguana, a dog, and some chatty birds. She sent me a photo of a magnificent white oak tree on her property. Its immense trunk is 14 feet around, and stands like a venerable guardian spirit in the mist, framed by two rainbows. "The first time we stepped into this house, we knew it was the right one. I often go out and sit by the tree and talk with it. I wonder how many Native Americans rested or camped under its canopy so many years ago.

"I got my first horses, Marti and Sunni, when I was fourteen. They were both half-Arabians. Marti was 4 when I got her and Sunni, Marti's foal, was born six months later. It was love at first sight. We spend many decades together. You can imagine how distraught I was when they passed on—Marti in 1992 at age 35 and Sunni in 1996 at age 30. They both died in the same way: they waited for me to get there, then they died with their heads in my lap. I somehow feel that they are now together.

"I still miss them terribly and I would spend hours in the evening sitting on a large glacial boulder we put over Marti's grave behind the barn.

"I once went to see a psychic. He said he could see a horse climbing steps, could see a horse in the house with me. And that's exactly what Marti did: she would come into the house looking for goodies.

"I now have two Arabians, Rocky and Kia. The last week of March, 1997, I put them out and was cleaning their stalls. When I finished, I called to them and could see that they were in the backyard by the garage.

"Come on, guys, let's go," I said. They both picked up their heads and looked at me. Normally they come running right in. Then I realized that my Rocky and Kia were actually in *front* of the barn, on the other side of the property—near Rt 4.

"Puzzled, I walked back into the barn and looked out to where I thought I had seen them before. In a flash, I saw Marti and Sunni standing together under the big oak tree. No doubt about it—it was them. My favorite horses in my favorite spot.

"I still get upset and cry, but it makes me feel better to know that they're still here. I'm never going to sell this place. I never want my Marti and Sunni to be disturbed."

THINGS THAT LURK IN THE LAKE

Loch Ness is the home of Nessie; Champ calls Lake Champlain home; Ogopogo swims the depths of Lake Okanagan. But Lake Erie may be the haunt of a monstrous serpent some call "South Bay Besse." I briefly mentioned the creature in the "Buckeye Bigfoots" chapter of *Haunted Ohio II*, only to find later that reports of giant snakes and lake lizards are amazingly common.

Reports of something eerie in Lake Erie go back to 1818 when Shubael West, master of the packet boat *Delia* described a monstrous sea-serpent attacking a whale [in a fresh-water lake?]. "The serpent's body was larger, in my opinion, than the mast of any ship I ever saw. Its tail appeared very ragged and rough and was shaped like an eel's and his head like that of a land serpent."

The original newspaper story, which supposedly appeared in the *Cleveland Gazette and Community Register* for July 31, 1818, I suspect was really an Atlantic Ocean story transposed to the lake, if not an outright hoax. The only thing that gives me pause is that (excluding the whale) the description sounds very much like the creature some boaters and skiers have seen in the last ten years.

The monster is said to be dark green or brown, 30 to 40 feet long and appears to undulate like a snake while swimming. No one has reported seeing all of its body exposed and no one has gotten close enough to tell whether the beast is scaly or slimy.[8]

John Schaffner, editor of the *Port Clinton Beacon*, started the recent flood of stories in the mid-1980s by reporting the claim of a woman who believed her dock was being rammed by a lake monster. It was actually a log, but Schaffner was deluged with calls from people who had seen *something* in the lake. Joking about the stories didn't dam the flood; even more came pouring in, some from very reputable witnesses.

A 40-foot boat pontoon washed up on Catawba Island in 1987. Skeptics proclaimed the mystery solved, but people continued to report strange creatures. As a joke, Schaffner's paper opened a toll-free monster hotline and ran a "name the monster" contest. The winner was "South Bay Besse," after the nearby Besse-Davis nuclear power plant at Oak Harbor. Tom Solberg, a marina operator and self-appointed Lake Erie monster folklorist, got local businesses to offer a $5,000 reward for the capture of the beast. Contestants had to produce a previously unknown Lake Erie creature, weighing at least 1,000 pounds, with a length of at least 30 feet. No one has collected the reward so far.[9]

Some say the monster is just floating logs; others suggest it might be a sturgeon magnified to monster proportions by the water or a group of sturgeon swimming nose to tail. The sturgeon is a plausible candidate—they can live to be over 100 years old and easily grow to a size of 10 feet long and 300 pounds. Some specimens are even larger. These monster fish are bottom feeders and are seldom seen on the surface.

It's also been suggested that the creature could be a zeuglodon or primitive whale, left over from the time when the dinosaurs ruled the waves. But Lake Erie is only about 12,000 years old—much too young a body of water for a saurian to have been trapped when the glaciers receded.

Besse could be waves breaking over a sand bar. Other explanations range from an ocean-going creature that slipped through the Welland Canal to rogue buoys or strings of floats to a freak wake from a freighter, or a mutant catfish from the waters near the nuclear power plant. Many of the Lake Erie monster reports come from east of the southwest lake islands. Sightings appear to increase in a dead calm. Cynics suggest that the island's wineries might have some bearing on the monster sightings.

Dr. Charles E. Herdendorf, professor emeritus of the Ohio State University Department of Zoology, has composed an impressive scientific name for Besse: *Vertebrate Chordata Ichthyoreptilia Obscuriformes Obscuridae Obscure eriensis huronii*, which, loosely translated, means "obscure Lake Erie life form."

"It's the job of scientists to explain it," Herdendorf said. "My personal view is that I'm skeptical, but I'm willing to be shown."

Herdendorf used a model designed to determine whether Loch Ness contained enough fish to support a monster the size of Nessie. The model revealed that Lake Erie has more than enough walleyes to feed up to 400 monsters of "Besse's" reported size.

In 1985 Demetrius Gooden of East Cleveland saw "something big and black" coming towards the boat when he was fishing for walleye with Frank Hughes. They were 25 to 30 miles offshore when they saw what looked like a "really long black alligator."[10]

In late summer, 1990, Bob Soracco, who had just moved to Ohio from Florida, was jet-skiing on the lake. He still had saltwater on the brain so when he saw a hump emerge from the water, he jetted over, thinking it might be a porpoise.

"I moved closer when I saw it surfacing. It looked like a porpoise, but bigger," he said, "But then I remembered where I was and got scared. I don't know what it was, but it was big, black, and had gray spots. I didn't have a drink in me," he said, "and I know what I saw."

Labor Day weekend of 1990, Harold Bricker of Shelby; his wife, Cora; and son, Robert, were fishing north of Cedar Point Amusement Park in Sandusky when a 35-foot black serpent-like creature swam by their boat. Five others, including a Huron firefighter, a Toledo angler, and a Pennsylvania grandmother, reported the same thing in September.

In all cases, the creature was reported to be about 35 feet long and black with a snakelike head. It surfaced in calm water in different places along the south shore between Toledo and Vermilion.[11]

In July of 1993, three boaters, in two separate incidents, saw the monster between Huron and Maumee Bay.

"I know what I saw," said John Liles, a Huron charter boat captain. "The thing is huge. I didn't see the head—just the tail flopping in the water toward the end of it." Liles and his wife, Holly, said they saw the snakelike creature about two miles from Kelleys Island while aboard their 52-foot charter boat.

Mrs. Liles described the serpent in great detail. It moved up and down, not side to side like a snake. It was black or dark brown and humped its body about 18 inches above the water.

From 175 to 200 feet away, they estimated its length to be about 15 to 25 feet.

Nine days earlier and about 10 miles away, a fisherman reported seeing a serpent measuring between 30 and 40 feet.[12]

Similar stories from different witnesses continue to surface over a decade. It makes you wonder if something besides zebra mussels** has slipped through the locks to haunt the lake. A lake called "Erie."

**Introduced to the lakes in boat ballast, these tiny creatures are wreaking ecological havoc by endangering native fish and mussel species, blocking water intake pipes, and damaging boats and docks.

POSSESSED POSSESSIONS*:
Objects with something extra

Death gave all that we possess.
-Thomas Hardy-

A CAUTIONARY TALE

Madge Bryan* was worried. Her elderly neighbor, Helena Phillips* was failing. Old Mrs. Phillips was in her 70s and, up until now, had lived by herself with no problems. But something had changed. It began when Mrs. Phillips told her neighbor that men who said they were from the gas company came into the house and stole things. Madge tried to soothe Mrs. Phillips, but she grew angrier and angrier and accused Madge of being in cahoots with the thieves. Next day, the elderly lady seemed to have forgotten all about it.

Then Mrs. Phillips began hearing voices. Staring intently at a point just below the ceiling, she'd listen and nod and respond, as if to questions. Once Madge overheard her saying, "If you think it's a good idea. I'm tired. You do what you want."

Every day Mrs. Phillips sat in her armchair in front of the TV. During *Wheel of Fortune* and *Jeopardy* she laid out game after game of solitaire on a board across her lap. Madge was helping the elderly woman, washing the supper dishes, when she heard a commotion from the living room. The cat streaked by, and she found Mrs. Phillips in a heap, surrounded by scattered playing cards and her lap board. "*&%$*! cat tried to

A tip of the hat to Ed Okonowicz whose book title I borrowed (see bibliography).

kill me," grumbled Mrs. Phillips . Madge helped her back to her chair and tried not to show her shock. Mrs. Phillips was a devout churchgoer and had never used any kind of coarse language before.

She dusted the old lady off and started stacking the cards on the board, which, now she saw for the first time had markings on the underside. She squinted at it, then turned it around. "Yes", "No", a sun, a moon, and the words "Ouija, Mystical Oracle" were printed on the board.

A Ouija board! Madge wanted to grab the board and run outside to the trash. Instead she said calmly,

"I think when you fell, the board bent so it won't fit across the arms of your chair any more. Should I find you a new one?"

"Stupid @#$% cat," Helena muttered. "Yeah, I guess you might as well get rid of the *&%$# thing."

With a sign of relief, Madge hurried the board out to the trash can at the curb. The next morning, the trash truck took it away.

And the next day Helena was back to her old, alert self—no voices, no visions, no paranoia. Just like that.

HEAR THE PENNIES DROPPING

When I was a child in Lutheran Sunday School, we sang a little ditty called "Hear the Pennies Dropping, Hear Them as They Fall," which is frighteningly appropriate for this tale of materializing money. Objects that appear out of nowhere are called "apports." I wrote about a few dollars of apporting pennies in *Haunted Ohio II*, but it's a real cash explosion in Greenville! Dave says his family received a windfall compliments of a generous ghost. They spent a week in Michigan on the funds they have received over the last three years from an apparition who leaves pennies in their home.

As soon as the family moved into their Greenville home, the pennies dropped: in the front entryway, in the upstairs hall, or the upstairs bedrooms.

At first, Dave suspected his teenage son J.C. of playing a prank, just to be irritating. But the contributions kept coming even after J.C. went away to the Navy. The family mentioned it to previous owners of the home. They too had been rattled by the spirit's spare change.

"I don't necessarily believe in this sort of thing, but after three years of unexplained instances it leaves questions in one's mind," Dave said.

The financial phantom also plays with the door leading to the third floor attic. It is normally kept locked with a deadbolt. But the door is often found open in the early morning hours. One former owner had the same experience and thought her kids were responsible. When she'd had enough, she slammed the door shut and yelled to the ghost, "Don't ever leave this door open again!" Her firmness paid off. The door stayed shut as long as she lived there. However, when Dave's family moved in, the door began opening again.

How do the pennies arrive? Dave told of a night when he and his wife were alone. At 4 a.m., they woke up simultaneously with a start. A moment later, they heard a penny hit the hardwood floor, spin, and roll.

Another time the ghost dropped a penny in the shower with Dave. "That shower curtain came open in a hurry!" Dave said. On still another occasion, his daughter, Erica, threw a penny up in the air. It never came down.

Pennies aren't the only things that drop. A young man who was staying with the family for a while gave Dave a yin-yang medallion to show his appreciation. The young man was playing the piano in the living room one day when the medallion flew through the air and hit him in the back. He stormed upstairs and confronted Dave. "Why did you throw it at me?" he demanded, hurt. Dave hadn't left the upstairs and he opened a drawer and showed the guest his original gift medallion, while the guest stared at the one that had just hit him on the back.

Dave's brother Dallas has seen the elusive penny-dropper. Dallas and Dave came back from an outing and while Dave went to the kitchen, Dallas waited behind him at the kitchen door. When he turned, the female ghost was standing directly behind him. She immediately turned, walked through the pocket doors from the living room to the dining room—only she didn't open the sliding pocket doors, just walked right through them. He didn't see her pass through them, but could hear her on the other side without the accompanying squeak of the doors opening.

He described her as about 5'3" tall, elderly, with grey hair. She looked perfectly real and solid. So real, in fact, that he asked his brother, "Who else is here?" On another occasion, Dave had a technician come to the house who got spooked by something standing behind him.

Dave explained that they had a spirit.

"Yes, I know," said the visitor. He described an elderly, grey-haired woman with a white persian cat who, he said, liked to sun himself in the window of the guest room. He also described the guest room, even though he had never seen it. Dave was taking it all with a grain of salt when the man added, "She wants you to know that the pennies are for luck."

That got Dave's attention. This was before anything had been written in the paper about the ghost or the pennies. The ghost has never done anything nasty. In fact, the family may owe their lives to her. The house's fuel-oil tank ran out and there was a small explosion, which just sounded like a pop to Dave. When he tried to get the furnace to start, it wouldn't. He called an electrician, who found that there was no power to the furnace starter. Tracing the wires into an old fuse box, Dave and the electrician found that *someone* had shut off the power on a previously unknown circuit.

There seems to be no pattern to the deposits. Months may go by without additional contributions. Family and friends think the spirit is a mixed blessing. They're a little uneasy about coming over to visit at night. But, they joke, if Dave could train the ghost to leave quarters or dollar bills, instead of pennies, the family could afford to go to Hawaii instead of the aptly-named Lake Erie.

THE PASTA-GEIST

In Singapore, one special month a year, hungry ghosts who have no living descendants to care for them are fed with lavish food offerings. If not appeased, they will wreak their vengeance on the living.

Closer to home, one woman found that her hungry ghost helped itself—all year round. In 1957, Carol and Doug Thornton got married while attending Bowling Green State University. They moved to the University Apartments in October, 1958 with a small baby in tow and another one on the way.

"That's where the macaroni mystery took place. I was alone much of the day because I had to drop my teaching job that year. That damned macaroni thing lasted the whole two years we lived there."

University Apartments started life as tar-papered barracks for G.I. reservist students. After the war, they were converted into somewhat shabby "married student" housing.

The Thorntons were glad of the low rent; money was tight even with the G.I. Bill paying for school. So they painted and hung curtains and tried to make the place livable. Curiously, they found that the apartment had been vacant for more than a year even with the housing shortage.

Their first week in University Apartments, Carol brought home the groceries including noodles, spaghetti, and macaroni, and started putting them on the kitchen shelves.

"I *know* I had macaroni because I lined it up on the shelf with the other pasta. But when I went to get it, the box was gone. Nothing but a blank space where it had been! I searched the cupboard but found no macaroni. So I cooked something else and kept quiet."

The next week Carol brought home two one-pound boxes of macaroni "to make sure." Again, they disappeared.

"I mentioned it to Doug after a while, thinking maybe he was trying to tell me he didn't like macaroni in any form. He was surprised, but he thought the whole thing was funny. It wasn't to me."

Carol set out to solve the case of the purloined pasta. She sifted through the garbage and looked under the car in case the pasta had fallen out of a shopping bag. Reaching for any solution, Doug and Carol wondered if a neighbor was sneaking in to play a practical joke on them. But doors and windows were locked and nothing in the apartment was ever disturbed. Carol reached a point where she started searching the *neighbors'* trash cans.

"I felt a compulsive need to find an answer, some kind of solution to the whole silly problem. If I could just find an empty box of the same brand of macaroni in a neighbor's trash I would say to myself, 'OK, so maybe they took it. That explains it so I won't mention it to anyone.' Eventually, at neighborhood cookouts, Doug mentioned the macaroni mystery. The neighbors thought it was hilarious. The macaroni kept coming up missing.

"Two or three times I came home and put the groceries on the kitchen table so I could take off my coat. Then I'd start the water boiling and reach for the macaroni—and it would have disappeared from the shopping bag! I swear, I think if ever I had thrown it into the water and watched it boil it still would have vanished before it was done!

"The macaroni itself finally became unimportant," she added, "The whole thing got to be a contest between me and whatever made the macaroni disappear. Every time ghosts and spirits popped into my mind I put them out. I just wanted to understand it—but I still don't. We lived there two years and the whole time we never had a meal with macaroni. And we must have bought more than 100 pounds of it."

One of the first meals the Thorntons had in their next home included macaroni and cheese. "We haven't been without macaroni since we left the University Apartments," said Carol.

I'm irresistibly reminded of the gobbling ghost in the first scene of *Ghostbusters* who would eat *anything*—even, possibly, raw macaroni![1]

THE FACE IN THE MIRROR

Belmont County was one of my "Dead Zones" counties where I've had difficulty tracking down stories. Then I heard from Matt, who lives in a 1920s house with his mother Vicki, his dad Gary, and sister Alitza. "We didn't notice anything right off," said Vicki "but there was a lot of remodeling being done. Once that was settled, things started happening."

The children had toy firetrucks with different buttons to push for different sounds: sirens, wooshing and whooping sounds.

"The ghost liked to push the buttons in the middle of the night! I'd yell downstairs, 'That's enough!' After I yelled, it would stop.

"We also heard footsteps on the stairs. I'd wake up and think, 'Did someone just come up the steps?' I'd walk out in the hall and there'd be nobody there. This only happened at night.

"In 1995 we had a psychic in the house. Before she left I said jokingly, 'Do you think we have a ghost?' She took it very seriously. 'You have three ghosts,' she said, indicating that there was an adult male, an adult female, and a young male ghost.

"We assumed our ghost was the boy. He was just playful and never caused any problems. Our neighbor, who is about 90 years old and remembers all sorts of local history, told us that in the early 1960s, a young boy, age 13 or 14, stood on a sawhorse in the garage and accidentally hung himself in some rope that had been hanging from a rafter. When we heard that, we thought maybe that's who it was. The kids have begun to call the ghost 'Herbert.'"

Certainly the ghost acts like a young prankster. Vicki's mom was doing laundry in the basement and someone kept flicking the lights on and off. She came upstairs and asked if the kids were playing tricks. The kids were all on an upper floor. So she went back down to finish the laundry and the lights began to flicker again.

"We had all the wiring replaced when we moved in, but we had it checked again. Nothing. Whatever it was loved to play with the lights in the rec room and the laundry area, but only during the day."

In April of 1997, Matt was reading in the living room. Their dog, Abby, was in her cage in the dining room. Matt's dad was downstairs in the rec room, asleep. At about 10 a.m. the sounds began.

It seemed like they were coming from the upstairs. Matt first noticed a sound like something clanging against the dog cage. The dog shot out of the cage and came to sit by Matt in the living room. She just wanted to be held and kept looking around and up towards the ceiling. Matt said, "I heard floorboards rattling, the sound of things shattering, broken glass, boxes being rattled around, metal clanging, things being knocked over. I couldn't call out to my dad. I was so scared, I couldn't *move*." Matt huddled there, clutching the dog, while the upstairs sounded like it was being systematically wrecked by vandals who didn't care how much noise they made.

After about an hour, the noises stopped and fifteen minutes later, Vicki came home from church to find her young son frozen in the corner, with the dog huddled next to him.

"He looked so pitiful, cowering in the corner," she said.

"What's knocked over?" he asked her and explained about the noises. "I was afraid to go see."

Vicki searched the whole house but, as is usual with this kind of noisy manifestation, everything was in order.

Abby, the family dog, seems to have scared off "Herbert." He hasn't played with the toys and Vicki hasn't heard footsteps since the family purchased the miniature schnauzer in the fall of 1996. Abby roams all over the house, but she does not like to go downstairs into the basement—where the lights still go on and off. Perhaps "Herbert" just got tired of hanging around upstairs or maybe he has made it clear to Abby where her territory ends.

In 1996, Vicki had her own strange experience with *something*. She had just finished her bath in the upstairs bathroom when the room began to fill with a white mist. It boiled thickly up out of nowhere. Although Vicki could see through it, she became quite alarmed thinking the brand-new hairdrier was on fire.

She turned the hairdrier off. Then she realized...

Her first reaction was to back up. "I opened the door to the bathroom and I said, 'This room's not big enough for the two of us!'"

At that, the strange white smoke dissolved; Vicki was alone again.

The most haunted thing in the house is the antique mirror that was left in the house by the previous owners. It now hangs in Vicki's office.

"There's a face on it," said Vicki. "Just a face. It measures about 8 inches tall. The face is dead in the middle of the mirror. It appears clearer when looked at from either side. We just dust around it."

A local art teacher made a sketch of the face, which Vicki faxed to me. It utterly unnerved me as it came through, line by line: first the broken-looking skull, then the hollow eye sockets—a scar running from cheekbone to the set mouth, and one blurry hand pressed against the glass of the mirror as if trying to get out.

The phantom who made the sounds of shattering glass and breaking furniture does not sound like a child ghost, nor does it fear the dog. Could the creature from the mirror have unleashed its malevolent energies to sweep through the house? If it is strong enough to do that, there is no telling what it could do, if it ever got out of that old and fragile mirror.

OH, SUSANNAH!

I first made the acquaintance of Dorothy Cox when she sent me her entire scrapbook of ghost-story clippings she had collected over the years. I was thrilled by her generosity! And now she has shared her own personal ghost story.

"Our brick house in Clyde was built before the Civil War by William Gillette, a bootmaker," she said, by way of introduction. "It's a strange old house."

Dorothy, her husband, and her family of three small children moved into the modest, two-story brick house in June, 1959. She had heard rumors of ghosts, but they only heard noises—muffled laughter, the rattle of china teacups, creaking stairs, doors closing. There was also a ghostly puppy. "We never saw it, of course. But we'd hear what sounded like a puppy scampering up the stairs. Or it would bump into the stove or a chair. We'd jump, then say,'Oh, that's just the puppy.'

After they moved in, Dorothy and her husband Bill were stripping off the horrible brown figured wallpaper prior to painting the living room a light grey. He was at one end of the room; she was at the other. Dorothy thought she heard something like a muffled giggle.

"Did you say something?" asked Bill.

"No, did you?" Dorothy said.

He hadn't and a moment later the silence was broken by a button from nowhere dropping between them, rolling, and falling to the floor. Dorothy picked it up. It was an old-fashioned, wooden sweater button. Neither could figure out where it had dropped from. Then there was another muffled giggle like they'd heard earlier.

"I believe the ghosts are letting us know they approve of our re-decoration," said Bill.

Her sister, in the teasing way of sisters, commented: "It means, 'Button your lip, Dorothy. You talk too much!"

The Coxes accepted their unseen guests with amused tolerance.

"The ladies are having a tea party," they'd say, whenever they heard the tinkling laughter and china cups rattling against saucers. The party sounds are always accompanied by a strong odor of an old-fashioned rose or lilac cologne, especially in the winter or fall when the house is closed up.

One day when daughter Louann was in the fifth grade, she was alone in the living room doing her homework. She looked up and in the doorway to the hall, she saw a tall woman in an old-fashioned white blouse and long skirt, hair on top of her head. The woman beckoned to her. Louann did what any intelligent person would do—she ran outside, terrified. She never saw the figure again.

A little later, Louann told her sisters and brother about the ghostly woman. Intrigued, they got out the Ouija board and started asking questions. The name "Sue" was spelled out, also "Susanna." They asked what Sue's occupation was. The Ouija board spelled out "schoolteacher."

Armed with these clues, Dorothy began checking around. She discovered that the house had once been owned by Miss Sue Heffner/Susannah J. Heffner, who taught fifth grade in the Clyde school between 1897 and 1906. Susannah's great-niece, now in her eighties, told Dorothy that the teacher had died in the Cherry Street house.

"I don't know whether it was Miss Sue, or the bootmaker's wife, or someone else who gave the tea parties. There haven't been any parties for a long time.

"However, this last year, I've had door openings and closings. When I went to bed and was just about to drop off to sleep, I heard a door close. I had checked earlier and could find no door problems. But again and again, as I was about to fall asleep, there it would go again. Open-creak-shut, open-creak-shut. Finally, I sat up in bed and said out loud, 'That is enough! Either leave the door open or shut. But leave it alone. I've got to get some sleep!' Then all was quiet. Maybe she just wanted to be noticed."

THE LAD WITH THE LAMP

"It's no Amityville," Bill Dixon admitted in a deep, comfortable voice when I interviewed him about the ghosts in the 1857 house he and his wife restored. It stands in Old Washington, a hamlet of about 300 souls in Guernsey County, the site of the northernmost battle of the Civil War. Morgan's

Raiders held the town for most of one day. Three of Morgan's men are buried in the local graveyard.

Built by Senator William Lawrence, the 17-room house has served as a rest home and a doctor's office. It stood vacant for quite some time before the Dixons bought it in 1979. It needed a lot of renovation and restoration. The Dixons took out patient cubicles and an enclosed stairway was opened up.

"It had been rented to lots of people," Dixon said, "Some told me, 'I rented that house and you'd never get *me* back in it!' How many people want to work on a wreck? It looked like heck. But we've mostly got it put back the way it was. We always got more interesting effects when doing remodeling.

"I've had some definite experiences. It was Christmas time and my wife was out at work. I was sitting in the library watching TV with the two dogs. I was sure I had locked the doors. I heard footsteps from the kitchen through the dining room, into the library and then I heard keys dropped and a glass set down. It wasn't my imagination—the dogs jumped off the couch, and ran to greet the visitor, assuming it was Ruth. They stopped and looked at the doorway, dumbfounded. Nobody had walked into the library; nobody else was in the house. That was the type of thing that happened to me."

Doors also open, especially one onto the upstairs porch, as Ruth Dixon can attest:

"We've got a double-decker screened-in porch on one side of house and one of the bedrooms opens onto the second level. When it's hot I'll sometimes go there to sleep. One night, it was so hot, I didn't fall right to sleep. I could hear footsteps coming towards the door to the porch. The door flew open and I looked up, expecting to see my husband.

"What's wrong?" I said.

"There was no one there and no one in the bedroom. Then I got to thinking. The bedroom is fully carpeted, I couldn't have heard anyone walking across it. I sat down in a chair. The door flew open again. It was a calm night and there was no wind. I stood up and said, "What seems to be the problem?" The door flew shut.

Both Bill and Ruth have heard mysterious sounds and footsteps. One day Ruth was chatting to a friend on the phone. "I was sitting in a chair beside the phone and as we talked, I could see the lights going on and off in the parlor through the transom over the door. I told my friend and she panicked! "You have seven or eight doors to the outside. You could have someone in there with you!"

"So I went to check. I couldn't get to the door with the transom because there was painting equipment piled in front of it, so I went up the hall to the other door. My two little dogs ran along with me. We were halfway up the hall when the door to the parlor flew open with a tremendous crash. We all stopped dead, then the dogs turned tail and ran. I heard quick footsteps—leather-soled shoes on wood—approaching out of the parlor and down the hall. I felt this cold breeze which got colder and colder the closer it got to me. I felt absolutely frigid, then the footsteps went on behind me, opened and shut a door that wasn't there. Then it was over. It was very, very scary. I really didn't know what to do.

"I went back to the phone and told my friend. She said to have the electricity checked and I imagined the rest. 'It's a dark, dreary day and you're alone in the house,' she said. 'Your weight on the floor caused the door to fly open.' But the door goes open all the time. The electricity was all fine.

"In the fall of 1979, we were still hard at work on the house doing major things like removing added walls. I was in the parlor with the door shut, the ladder in front of it, preparing the plaster for paint.

"Now I absolutely loathe our basement—that dungeon of terror! It has this eerily trickling spring. I get nervous whenever I or anybody else has to go down there. Bill was down there and I kept peeking through the transom since I was 11 feet up the ladder and I could see into the kitchen where the basement steps were. I saw a little boy standing in the doorway of the kitchen.

"Oh no," I thought "another child has gotten in. My husband's left the door open!" I was concerned because we

had paints and stripper chemicals and a lot of things unsafe for
kids. I got off the ladder, moved it aside, and opened the door.
I could still see the little boy, but much clearer now.

"He was a young black child about eight or nine years old,
less than 4 foot tall. He wore bib overalls with no shirt and he
was barefoot. He had a tremendous mop of long curly hair. In
his hands he was holding a huge kerosene lantern. He held it
straight out in both arms and it partially covered his face. I
didn't get the feeling he could see me.

"'Where did a child find a lantern like that?' I thought to
myself. I took two or three steps and I could start to see through
him. I remember noticing the kitchen cabinets behind him. I
took one more step and he completely disappeared.

"What gets even stranger is, within a minute or so, I was
standing staring at the doorway when Bill came up from the
basement. 'You'll never believe what I just found!' he said. He
had part of a rusted lantern and the bottom was exactly like the
one the child was holding. The top was gone, but it was
huge—about 14 inches in diameter. We showed it to a local
museum curator and we were told it was a meeting house
lantern.

"She had me chasing all over the house," said Bill "If there
had been a kid, he would have had a hard time getting in
without being heard. The dogs would have barked; they were
noisy little critters. The house is supposed to have been used at
the time of the Underground Railroad. According to local
tradition, a sick runaway slave died here. Because the house is
so close to the neighbors' house, they couldn't bury him in the
daytime. He was buried after dark in the side yard. But this is
just hearsay."

Records do show that during William Lawrence's owner-
ship he employed up to four black servants, including a Mrs.
Ransom and her son Revedy.

"We do have three hidden rooms," Ruth added. "We
suspect that there's a tunnel, but we haven't had the nerve to go
dig."

I asked Ruth if she'd ever experienced anything she'd call a time-warp. "Oh yes, one summer day in 1981 as I was working in the flowers, I just sat down on the grass to rest for about 20 minutes. There's normally lots of traffic, but that day it was quiet. Sitting there, it was so warm and peaceful, with the bees buzzing.

"All of a sudden I could hear what sounded like hooves hitting the pavement and leather creaking slowly. It immediately caught my attention because it was so unexpected and seemed extremely close and clear. I thought it was some Amish people in a buggy. I looked up to Main Street, the Old National Road, that runs in front of our house. I saw a team of two oxen coming up the street with a tall wagon behind them loaded with what seemed to be bags. There was a man walking behind the wagon, but I didn't notice a driver. 'Well, that's interesting,' I thought, 'the Amish must have oxen.'

"Then I realized that, whatever I was seeing, the house across the street, which had been built in 1848, wasn't there. This startled me and I jumped. When I jerked, everything went back to normal: the house across the street was back, and the oxen were gone."

Ruth thinks that their primary ghost might be Congressman Lawrence, keeping an eye on things. But there could be more than one ghost. Supposedly one of Lawrence's young daughters died in the house after going insane.

"We also have music in the parlor on a regular basis," said Bill. "From a distance, it sounds like a music box; closer, it's tinny like a harpsichord. You can check outside and all through the house, but you don't hear it anywhere but in the parlor. The dogs will sit in the door and watch while it's going on. Lawrence, the man who built the house, *did* play the harpsichord and held musical evenings in the parlor.

"I frequently say its a time warp," added Ruth. "Once when I walked past the parlor door and heard music, I stopped and looked in. The music quit immediately. Then I heard footsteps and it sounded like a man walking across the floor with a lighter person walking behind him. I thought, 'I haven't heard *that* before.' I walked into the parlor; it stopped. I walked back out, it started again. Then I heard *three* sets of footsteps, the man's heavy ones, some medium ones, and the light ones. I got to experimenting with it, coming in a different door, each time. There were footsteps each time, usually two or three sets.

"I could practically see them sitting there in the 1860s, saying to each other, 'Did you just see a woman coming through here in pants?' Maybe to them, *we* are the ghosts."

THESE LEGS ARE MADE FOR WALKING

Frances loved to go to garage sales. She and her husband would drive over to Lancaster from their Pike County home and spend the day with her brother Paul and his daughter Karen, driving around looking for bargains. At one sale, Frances' husband bought a shotgun and Frances bought a long strip of rug for the hallway. It had a large dirty-looking blotch on it, but Frances was sure she could scrub it clean.

She laid it out in the sun and scrubbed away, first with plenty of lye-soap, then with detergent, but each time the rug dried the spot came back, big and ugly as ever. She glared at it. It looked like a pool of something liquid—oil maybe?—had oozed out onto the rug. One part of the spot stuck out, like an arm. Irritated, Frances put the rug in their hallway. She was going to get her money out of that rug if it killed her!

The next night Frances' husband was watching TV when he caught a glimpse of something moving in the hall. Curious, for Frances was in bed and they didn't have any pets, he leaned over to see what it was, and nearly fell out of his chair.

It was a pair of legs, walking up and down the hall. They wore long gray men's socks with the red stripe at the top, like the kind used to make sock-monkeys. They paced up and down that rug, tapering off into a misty nothingness about mid-thigh.

He said nothing about it until one night he returned from a meeting to find a white-faced Frances sitting outside on the porch. The couple compared notes: each had seen the ghostly pair of legs.

Everyone in their family laughed at them when they heard about it—until Frances' grandson Randy saw the legs while staying the night. So another grandson, Dale, named the spook "Fred."

Why just legs? the couple wondered. And that spot on the rug—was it blood? Was someone killed and hacked to pieces and the pieces rolled up in the carpet?

"We've got to get rid of that rug," Frances' husband said, finally. Frances rolled it up and tied it with twine and stowed it in the garage until trash day. That night there was a terrible crash in the garage, like a dozen cement blocks had fallen on the roof. They didn't dare go out to see what had happened.

On trash day, the garbage collector was thrilled to find a nice carpet runner and he put it up front with him.

"I wonder how long *he* kept it?" Frances mused later. Just to be on the safe side, her husband sold the shotgun. And the phantom legs never walked again.[2]

THEY'RE BAAAACK!:
Return to *Haunted Ohio*

O lost, and by the wind grieved,
ghost, come back again.
-Thomas Wolfe-

After I wrote the first book in the *Haunted Ohio* series, I began to get letters from readers who knew more stories about the places I cited. Return with me now, to see what's been going on at some of these haunt-spots.

THE GREY LADY OF THE
CONFEDERATE CEMETERY

Haunted Ohio, p. 46

In *Haunted Ohio*, I told of the weeping "Grey Lady." I discovered that a living lady had once haunted the cemetery and apparently continues to haunt it after death. But who was she?

Camp Chase, on Livingston Avenue in Columbus, served as a prison-camp for Confederate soldiers. It was as bad as most prison camps of the time and some 2,000 Confederate prisoners died there of disease and malnutrition. Many were buried in the prison cemetery.

After the War, the cemetery fell into disrepair and that's where we find our first possible candidate for the Grey Lady.

Louisiana Ransburgh, named for her southern mother's home state, loathed Yankees. John Ransburgh, her father, owned a plantation near New Madrid, Missouri. When Union troops occupied New Madrid, he sent the teenaged Louisiana away to boarding school at Ohio Wesleyan in Delaware, north of Columbus where Ransburgh had relatives..

At school, Louisiana carried in her own stool—so she wouldn't have to share a bench with those "dirty Black Republicans," as she so tactfully called her fellow classmates. When Lincoln was assassinated, Louisiana publicly rejoiced in the streets of Delaware, nearly getting herself lynched by angry mourners.

So it was the ultimate irony when this young Yankee-hater fell in love with a northerner, Joseph Briggs, a wealthy farmer with a large estate on what is now the Hilltop on the west side of Columbus. They married in 1867 and settled very near the site of the prison cemetery.

There the weeds grew high and covered the remains of the rotting wooden markers. Her neighbors were mostly former Union soldiers. Even her husband had been a captain in the Ohio militia. Yet she still felt a need to show her sympathies for the south. Wearing a heavy veil to conceal her face, Louisiana Briggs would slip into the cemetery at night with flowers which she spread over the weed-covered ground. Sometimes all she could do was toss the flowers over the crumbling cemetery fence, built out of wood from the former prison barracks. Could the Grey Lady be Louisiana Ransburgh Briggs who is still paying her respects to her fallen southern brethren?[1]

Today the cemetery occupies a space about the size of a football field. Row upon row of identical grave markers line up like dominos within the stone-walled enclosure. In some places the stones are so close together you cannot walk between them.

On October 31, 1991, I was scheduled to broadcast from the cemetery for Channel 6's Noon News. For their Halloween show, they wanted a shot of the grave where flowers mysteriously appear—that of Benjamin Allen of the 50th Tennessee Volunteers. I had never been to the cemetery before so I arrived a little early, thinking that I'd locate the grave and be ready when the TV crew arrived.

The metal gate of the cemetery groaned stiffly as I opened it. It was a chill, overcast day. I wore an 1860s black silk shawl from my collection of vintage clothing, hoping that it might provoke an appearance by the Grey Lady. I looked at the hundreds of tombstones in dismay.

How in the world was I going to find one particular grave among the rows of identical markers? I had about five minutes before the TV crew was to arrive. A local historian had promised to drop by with some maps, but I couldn't wait for her. Suddenly I remembered a tip from my friend Rosi Mackey, who frequently visits cemeteries for genealogical research.

When she visits an unfamiliar cemetery, she calls out, "So-and-so, where are you?" Then she finds that she can walk directly to the grave. She swore by the technique.

What the heck, I thought, what have I got to lose?

"Mr. Allen," I said mentally "Where are you?"

Then I set out strolling between the tombstones towards an open space at the west end of the cemetery. At one point, the thought popped into my head: If I turn around, I'll see the grave. I turned slowly to my left. And there it was, the tombstone of Benjamin Allen, 50th Tennessee Volunteers. Out of several hundred graves, I had found it on my first try. Pure luck, perhaps. Or perhaps I was graciously escorted by a shadowy figure in grey.

TRACKING DOWN THE LINCOLN GHOST TRAIN

Haunted Ohio, p. 106

In *Haunted Ohio*, I reported the story that Lincoln's funeral train retraces its melancholy route from Washington, D.C. back to Illinois in the month of April. *Columbus Dispatch* writer and ghostlore afficionado John Switzer wrote in his April 6, 1995 column that folks were heading out to the tracks to track down the apparition.

1995 marked the 130th anniversary of the funeral train's visit to Columbus. Even more significantly, the exact days of the week corresponded with the days in 1865. Lincoln was shot on Good Friday—April 14—which was also Good Friday in 1995. The train arrived in Columbus on Saturday, April 29, 1865, and April 29 fell on a Saturday in 1995.

Colonel Crawford School history teacher Mark Cory handed out copies of Switzer's column. About fifty of his students, their parents, and other North Robinson residents, went out to keep the vigil at midnight on the Friday "anniversary." They didn't see anything. But someone else did.

Beth and her friend Dawn had never heard the story of the ghost train. At 10:30 p.m. Saturday, they were on their way home after having dinner. As they approached the tracks, the flashers at the railroad crossing on Parcher Road were not flashing. But as Beth drove towards them, she saw the approaching headlights of a train. Sensibly, she didn't try to beat it across. Instead she waited, and she waited. And as she watched, the train light suddenly disappeared.

"I never saw anything like it," she said. "It was very strange. I try not to believe in this stuff. But when you can't explain it...."[2]

THE GHOSTS OF SINCLAIR

Haunted Ohio, p. 144
Haunted Ohio II, p. 144

Students and staff at Sinclair Community College have frequently reported sightings of ghosts. One of them, a relative newcomer, is known as "Mr. Joshua." He has been sighted, appropriately enough, in Building 13, formerly the site of United Color Press. According to legend, a worker caught his arm in a press and bled to death there. Some of the ghostly activity is attributed to the unfortunate worker..

"The building is very uneasy," admitted Julie*, a member of the security staff at Sinclair. "When I was a Sinclair security officer, I saw someone looking out of one of the upper windows of Building 13. Sinclair officers covered the entrances and Dayton police came in to help with the building search. We chased an older white male with grey hair, dressed in old jeans and a shirt—and he went right through a wall. Three of us saw him. We couldn't believe it!

"'Did you guys see where he went?' I said.

"'I saw where he went and I'm not going to talk about it!' another officer said gruffly. 'You're not going to get me into this building again!'

"We reported the building clear and left."

Another time Julie took a utility worker in to look at the generators. "I heard something. He and I both saw a little old man with what looked like a mule. Man and mule vanished by the freight elevator."

Before the Color Press structure was built, the area was reportedly the site of a railroad roundhouse. Perhaps that's where the man with the mule comes in. Others believe he perished in the great 1913 flood.

Criss, a secretary at Sinclair, believes she also saw Mr. Joshua. While she was at her desk, she saw an old man in overalls standing on the other side of the room. Assuming he was a student, she said she'd be with him in a minute and stepped behind a pillar for a few seconds. When she stepped out again, she found that he was gone. She opened her office door and looked both ways down the long corridor. She saw no one.

A few days later, Renee, an Applied Arts lab technician, was in her office printing a long document. As usual, the first page was on her computer screen. She busied herself with other work and when the document was finished printing, she found the word "Joshua" printed on the first page in bold capital letters about an inch high.

She hadn't seen the name on her computer screen and neither had another instructor who had been in her office when she started printing. It is possible that someone playing a prank could have put the name into a header file. Renee says it doesn't seem like a prank a faculty member would play. But the prankster may have been a less "solid" citizen.

Julie said that she's also had strange experiences in Blair Hall, on Sinclair's main campus.

"One summer we were having a concert in Blair Hall, where the air conditioning was malfunctioning. After everyone left, we went to lock up the revolving door. All of a sudden the lights went on and off by themselves and a really cold, cutting wintery wind went by. We heard a snap. The locking bolts to the revolving door came up and the door started spinning. Whatever it was, it's got a *lot* of energy."[3]

WOODLAND CEMETERY

Haunted Ohio, p. 67

The Ghostly Girl of Woodland Cemetery

Dayton's Woodland Cemetery is dotted with the graves of the dead and famous. Some of Dayton's most distinguished decedents lie here: the Wright Brothers and their sister Katherine, poet Paul Lawrence Dunbar, John H. Patterson, the founder of NCR, and Lib Hedges—Dayton's most notorious madam.

It is also home to one of Dayton's most famous ghosts, the ghostly girl of Woodland Cemetery, which I wrote about in *Haunted Ohio*. After that book came out, I heard more about her from a young man named Dan.

In the mid-1960s, Dan had been placing flowers on a grave. He spent some time there and as he was turning away from the grave to his car, he heard a woman weeping bitterly. He looked around him. There was no one there to account for the sounds. Finally, baffled, he gave up looking, although the crying was quite loud.

As he got back in his car, he felt something in the car with him. He sensed it was a young woman. She was sobbing inconsolably in the seat beside him. He wanted to comfort her, but how do you help someone you can't see?

The spirit cried all the way back to his house then followed him up onto the porch of his house and stood outside the screen door, weeping as if her heart would break.

The young man's grandmother heard the noise and said knowingly, "You've brought home a spirit." Dan doesn't know what she did, but his grandmother somehow got rid of the ghost, who has since been seen back at the cemetery. I wonder if the ghostly girl hitched a ride back to Woodland. If so, we may hear of another vanishing hitchhiker story soon.

A Sealed Vault Mystery

When I asked a Woodland Cemetery manager if he knew any ghost stories, he chuckled and told me the following tale:

One morning the groundskeepers heard screaming coming from the old, unused holding vault—this was an above-ground temporary tomb to hold the coffins of people who died when the ground was too frozen to dig out a grave. It was designed in the "Theban" or Egyptian style and it looks quite eerie with its massive columns looming out of the hillside.

At any rate, the workers heard somebody yelling from inside the vault. Peering through the grate, they saw an old drunk who had spent the night in the vault and had just now realized where he was. Talk about feeling like death warmed over.... The funny thing was, they couldn't figure out just *how* the man had gotten into the vault. They had to use a torch to cut through the metal gates of the only entrance—which had long ago rusted shut.

Little Boy Lost

One of Woodland Cemetery's more poignant monuments is that of Johnny Morehouse. A massive dog drapes a paw protectively over the sleeping boy. At his feet there lies a ball, a harmonica, a top, and a boy's cap. There is no date or epitaph except "slumber sweet." On any day you can see flowers or small toys that have been left on the grave.

On June 7, 1997, a man living near Woodland was sitting on his porch enjoying the early evening calm. He could see above Shelton's Pharmacy through the trees to the mausoleum on the hill. There, he was startled to see a little boy—three or four years old, dressed in old-fashioned knickers, accompanied by a dog, wandering between the graves. Although it wasn't dark yet, the cemetery gates had been closed for the night. He watched the child long enough to realize that no adult was with him. He immediately sent his grandson through the cemetery fence to fetch the child. The boy returned, confused. He couldn't find a trace of the little boy or his dog.

The Dayton Police brought in a dog and a tracker; they were that concerned that there might be a lost child wandering the cemetery. The only thing found was an old bicycle helmet that looked like it had been there a long time. The police dog never picked up a scent to follow.

The police called for Hamilton's helicopter, which is equipped with sophisticated infrared nightvision that reacts to body heat. They ran a grid search but found nothing. If a living boy and his dog been there, some trace would have been found. A police officer told me that even a newly-dead body holds enough heat to be detected for some time after death by the equipment.

I visited the Morehouse monument on a calm day and noticed something strange. The dog's stone nostrils are deeply drilled. If you hold your hand beneath them, you can feel warm air, as if the dog still breathes.

It's probably just some trick of porous stone and changing air temperatures. But I wonder if the first place the police should have looked was the pedestal of Johnny's statue. Would they have found it empty? Or would they have found a sleeping stone boy and an out-of-breath stone dog?

ALICE THE GHOSTLY ACTRESS

Haunted Ohio, p. 51

Alice, the ghostly actress of Bowling Green's Joe E. Brown and Eva Marie Saint Theatres, is still on the job. I spoke at the Eva Marie Saint Theatre during a Power of the Pen regional competition in October of 1996. I jokingly asked the people arranging the event if they had invited Alice, who is known to cause trouble if not properly invited to all events held in the theatre. No one had.

Just before I went on, one of the organizers pulled me aside and said, "Stall as long as you can. Our computers have all gone down and we can't tabulate the results of the competition!" Alice had struck again!

Alice showed herself to stage manager Marcia Miller in the spring of 1992. One of Miller's friends invited Alice to a production in a nearby theatre. Miller says she felt like Alice was not where she was supposed to be. Miller went to a staircase backstage and there she saw Alice.

"At first she tried to scare me. She 'threw a face' at me, like in *Ghostbusters* and my heart stopped... I told her that my friend was downstairs inviting her to their show. That was the person Alice needed to talk to."

Reportedly, Alice dresses in '20s style clothing, but Miller does not want to describe what she saw. Out of respect for Alice, she remains wary of giving people something to look for—something to talk about.

Although she claims she was chased out of the building earlier in the semester by a "bad" spirit, Miller says she is not afraid to be in the theatre building alone. However, she thinks someone may have spoken badly of Alice because a recent production of *Henry IV* was plagued with difficulties. Two actors suffered injuries in the final weeks of rehearsal, props fell off the wall, and on one performance night, the box office computers were down.[4]

THE HEADLESS CONDUCTOR OF MOONVILLE

Haunted Ohio, p. 92

Students at Ohio University in Athens know that Moonville is the site of Raccoon Creek swimming hole, one of the area's prime skinny-dipping spots. It is also the name of a ghost town—a former mining and railroad town that has left behind no trace except the eerie Moonville tunnel.

The mouth of the tunnel overlooks the swimming hole. An abandoned trestle spans the creek leading into the tunnel. Swimmers often dive into Raccoon Creek from the trestle's end or swing from a rope tied to a nearby tree.

One night several years ago, David and a group of friends headed for Moonville. They swung on the rope, swam in the water and drank a few beers. Then they gathered up their gear and began trudging up the hill to their car which was parked on the other side of the tunnel.

The air in the tunnel, David recalls, was icy cold after the balmy night breeze. Utter blackness swallowed them as they passed through the tunnel's rounded arch. Once inside, they saw somebody coming through the tunnel with what looked like a flashlight.

Since the group had beer with them and some of the group were under age, they split up—half going forward to face the flashlight carrier, the others retreating to hide the beer. The next thing David remembers, the group that had gone forward suddenly turned around and "passed us running. They yelled back, 'There's no one carrying the light!'"

A skeptical David went to check it out himself. "[My friend] wasn't kidding," he says. "It was just a swinging light with no one holding it. I hightailed it back to the car. I haven't been out there since."[5]

THE GHOSTS OF THE AIR

Haunted Ohio II, p. 163

The ghosts of the air are still flying high at and around the United States Air Force Museum in Dayton.

Scary in Pinks

Patrick*, who saw the ghostly girl of Woodland Cemetery, (See *Haunted Ohio*) was working for a local police force. The local force had a reciprocal aid agreement with nearby Wright-Patterson Air Force Base so when, about 2 a.m., he and his partner heard a call about an intruder at the Visitor's Center, they drove onto the base.

"The tornado alarm went off. I thought the aliens had got loose or terrorists were storming the base. Nobody could explain why the alarm went off."

The duo pulled up to the Visitor's Center, located in a quonset hut.

"There was a guy standing there, behind the hut. And he *waved* at me. I asked the dispatcher if there were any base cops in the area. 'No,' he said, 'they're still in the museum building.'

"Now I'm something of a military buff and I could see that the man had on what are called 'pinks.' This was a dress uniform worn by junior and senior grade pilots during World War II. He also had on an overseas cap, not a camo cap like a regular military cop. He saluted. I got out of my car with my flashlight and as soon as the light hit him, he disappeared."

The Vanishing Mechanic

I received this story in 1992 after *Haunted Ohio II* came out. I thank the person who sent it and remind him to call me when he retires and doesn't have to worry about his security clearance so I can put his name in the next printing of the book. This is his story.

In the fall of 1967, I was a young engineer, fresh out of college, working on a project I was sure was the most important in the Air Force. Still being relatively new in town, my social life was nothing to write home about, and I frequently worked late. One Friday, I decided to stay late and finish up some loose ends, and before I knew it, it was almost eight o'clock. Heading out for home, I drove up the then active Wright Field flight line as I often did, being the airplane nut I am. As I approached one of the hangers which now houses the Air Force Museum restoration area, I saw a man in coveralls run from behind a C-47 toward the hanger. Although it was almost dark, I could see he was in a hurry and seemed quite upset. As he entered the beam of my headlights, he suddenly stopped and waved me down, pointing toward the airplane.

Thinking someone must have been injured while doing late evening maintenance on the flight line, I stopped to offer my help. As I got out of my car, the man was still standing and waving, and appeared to be yelling something, but I could hear no sound whatsoever. I shouted to him to ask what was the matter, but he turned tail and sprinted back toward the airplane. The combination of his head start and the non-athletic qualities of my wing-tips kept me a good 15-20 yards behind until he got to the airplane.

As he reached the aircraft, he simply disappeared! No sliding under the airplane or even fading out, this guy flat vanished right before my eyes.

Being absolutely terrified, I did an about face, ran back to my old Chevy, and "got the Hell out of Dodge." When I went back to work on Monday, the C-47 was gone, apparently having flown out over the weekend....

The C-47s had been in the Air Force's inventory since before World War II, and many WWII, Korea, and Vietnam veteran aircraft of that type were still flying in 1967. Had this man been seeking help for an injured buddy of a war or accident from years past? I never asked around the old maintenance shops to see if anyone had ever seen anything unusual, nor had I ever heard of any such occurrence on base until I overheard two women discussing your [Air Force Museum] stories.

And my question is: Did that C-47 *really* fly out over the weekend? Or did it take off into some other dimension?

THE GHOSTS OF THE BUXTON INN

Haunted Ohio II, p. 17

My daughter and I were doing a book fair in Granville and on a whim, I decided to see if the Buxton Inn had any rooms left. "*Don't* put me in the haunted room," I said to the clerk. "Don't even put me in the haunted *building*." So we were given a lovely two-bedroom suite with a sitting area in one of the guest houses at the end of the block.

"This is better than staying at the White House," exclaimed my daughter, who has always loved historic buildings. I had not told her anything about the ghosts at the Buxton and I was curious to know what she would sense about the Inn. In our room, she didn't really have much to say except she insisted I stay with her during her bath, something she hadn't wanted for years. Later she said she felt like someone else was there, but "it didn't really register that it was a ghost."

I tucked her in and read a little, then quickly fell asleep. About three in the morning, I was suddenly awakened by the sense that someone was in the room with me. I sat bolt upright in a cold sweat, my heart pounding. There, sitting in the wing chair, across the room from me, was Major Buxton. He wore a natty, white summer suit and a big smile. He had apparently just come to pay a social call. I guess the dead don't know what time it is.

"You're scaring me," I said to him. "*Please* go away."

He smiled graciously—and disappeared. I was so rattled, I had to turn on the light and read for an hour before I could sleep again.

The next morning we went down to breakfast in the Greenhouse Room. Several grilled trout and waffles later, we waddled up to the front desk and asked if we could just wander around. It was only about 8 a.m.; so of course, none of the bars were open. We started down the steep stairs into the Tavern Room where I had seen a rough-looking, ghostly man standing by the bar on a previous visit. The room had originally been the place where coach drivers ate and slept. My daughter got halfway down the steps and stopped dead.

"I can't go down there, Mom," she said, "There are people down there." She retreated into the hall and I walked further downstairs to see. The Tavern Room was empty—of any human life. She described feeling "roughish" men having a drink. "When I went down there, it wasn't morning any more. It felt like it was night," she said.

Perhaps for the rowdy drovers tossing down just one more for the road, it still is.

9

THE GHOSTLY MISCELLANY:
A potpourri of poltergeists

A spirit passed before my face;
the hair of my flesh stood up.
-Job 4:15-

THE BLUE LIGHT SPECTRE

I first met Mindy when she auditioned as a tour guide for my Dayton Ghost-Bus Tours. Applicants were asked to improvise a ghost story and Mindy, a self-assured student at Wright State, didn't flinch: she had her own personal tale to tell.

Mindy lived in a double on Smithville, in the Belmont area of Dayton. In 1989, Mindy's mother was painting in the front bedroom when, out of the corner of her eye, she saw something move in the hall. Naturally she thought it was Mindy or one of her three roommates and called out to them. Nobody answered and she went back to painting. Again, she caught a glimpse of somebody in the hall. She also smelled a strong smell of electric burning, like ozone just after lightning strikes. Mindy and her roommates, Scott, Amy and Jolie, were not in the house.

A few days later, Mindy's mother was putting on the second coat of paint when, again, something moved in the hall. She turned quickly, just in time to see blue smoke. That's when she had the landlord call in an electrician who gave the house a clean bill of electrical health.

Mindy's cousin Scott was the only male living in the house. He was in the shower upstairs when he heard the bathroom door open. Thinking it was one of his roommates, he called a warning, "I'm in here." Nobody said anything back. He pulled back the shower curtain, but he was alone. Or so he thought.

He went back to his shower, when someone started poking at him through the curtain.

"C'mon, you guys," he said, "cut it out." He yanked back the curtain with irritation, but nobody was there. "OK," he said to himself, "the window's open and the curtain blew." He reached over and shut the window. Feeling a little chilly, he turned up the hot water in the shower.

Then his blood ran cold as the poking began again. Poke, poke, poke, the invisible finger stabbed at the curtain. This time he grabbed at the finger and came up with shower curtain. Ripping back the curtain, he found himself staring at the hardwood door of the bathroom. For the first time, he noticed the shape of a person in the wood grain. There was the outline of a woman: a head, her arms, raised, as though they were reaching out, a small waist, and hips defined to just below the waist. "I never noticed *that* before, he thought uneasily.

"He moved out a week later," Mindy commented ruefully. "He was always the biggest chicken. He told us about it and we said, 'yeah, yeah...' Before that, we'd had the usual lights flickering and TV going on and off. I thought it was just my housemates trying to spook each other, until one night I got home at 2:30 a.m. from my waitress job.

"I saw that Amy's bedroom light was on. I went upstairs and knocked on her door but there was no answer. I looked in; she wasn't there. Her room looked like it always did—bed unmade, work clothes flung on a chair. So I turned out the light and went downstairs.

"Then I heard furniture moving. 'Is Scott rearranging his furniture?' I wondered as I walked back upstairs. But his door was shut. Then I heard a thump in Amy's bedroom. When I looked in there, it was a mess! Her clothes were all out of the closet. It looked like it had been ransacked. 'Oh my God,' I thought, 'is there somebody trying to rob our house?'

"I heard Jolie come in downstairs and I went running down there. 'I think something weird is going on here,' I told her. 'Amy's room is a mess.'

'Well, that's not unusual,' said Jolie.

"I explained and she went upstairs with me to look. The room was back to the way it was before.

'Well, this isn't *that* big a mess,' said Jolie as I gawked. All the clothes that had been out of the closet were back in."

Back downstairs Mindy began to freak out. She heard more noises and ran upstairs with Jolie behind her. Amy's room was just as it had been a few minutes before. But Mindy's attention was arrested by something down the hall near her room.

There, like a flickering, old-time movie, floated a young woman, from the hipbones up. Only she was blue—all different shades of blue: deep midnight for her Gibson Girl hair, pale blue for her skin; light blue for her high-collared shirtwaist blouse held at the throat by a brooch, gas-flame blue for her belt that circled a very small waist. All was blue and smoky around her and Mindy could smell that burning, electric smell.

The blue lady looked at Mindy for about five seconds and held her arms straight out, palms up, as if in appeal. The living and the dead locked eyes for a few brief seconds and Mindy says it was as if the blue lady was searching for recognition. Then the blue ghost covered up her face, fingers on her forehead, looking down. Next she turned left so Mindy and Jolie could see her profile, and she walked through the wall.

The two women stared, their mouths open, eyes wide with shock. Scott came out of his room just as the blue lady vanished through the wall. All three smelled the electric smell.

"Needless to say, we all spent that night at my mother's!

"You know" said Mindy, "I was never afraid of her. I never felt that she was a bad or mean person, I thought she was sad. That was the only time I saw her."

Mindy's friend Mike frequently came over to study. He was sitting in the kitchen when he heard somebody in hard-soled shoes click-clacking down the back stairs to the basement. He went downstairs and there he too smelled the lightning-strike smell. He came back upstairs and went back to studying, when he heard the footsteps coming *up* the stairs.

He looked out the window to see who was coming out, then he saw her standing behind him at the window. He only caught a glimpse of a woman dressed in Victorian clothes—a *blue* woman. He turned around and she was gone, leaving the smell of brimstone.

Mindy moved out shortly after that for financial reasons, but she's always wondered about the blue lady. Why blue? Was she unhappy? Did she burn to death in the house?

"I thought it was interesting that you always smelled that burning smell, that she was blue like a gas flame, and that Scott found those burnt matches in the basement.

"I found out years later that one of the reasons Scott moved out was that in the basement, where he stored stuff, he found nine burnt wooden matches arranged in three triangles, which in turn were arranged in a bigger triangle.

"'That's kind of weird,' he thought, and picked them up and threw them away. He went back down to the same spot a few days later; there they were again. This time Scott marked one of them, and threw them away. When he went down a couple days later, he found the same triangles, including the marked match."

Maybe Scott wasn't such a chicken, after all.

PRISCILLA OF PRESCOTT HOUSE

It was a dark and stormy night. Dr. Robert Haas* was up on the lonely third floor of Prescott* House, closing and latching the last of the storm windows just as the rain hit.

Afterwards, he found his wife Lisa on the second floor staring out the window. "Bob, did we do the right thing...moving here, I mean? It's like this house belongs to a different time. I get this weird feeling the house is somehow *rejecting* us."

"Rejecting us?" Haas said lightly, "We're not an organ transplant! Hey, we've only lived here two weeks. Give it a chance."

Lisa smiled and hugged her husband. As she looked past his shoulder, her body stiffened.

"Bob! Look!"

He spun around to see a miniature waterfall flowing down the stairs from the third floor.

"Where is it coming from? Is the roof leaking?"

Bob shook his head. "It would take a hole the size of a basketball to let in that much water." He ran up the stairs and walked into a storm on the third floor. Water whirled everywhere while the wind shredded the sheer white curtains. Every window on the third floor was wide open.

Bob struggled to close and latch them. He was almost finished when he heard a female voice call above the howling wind, "STOP!"

Bob froze, "Stop?" he repeated, "You want the house to wash away, Lisa?" He latched the last window and picked his way down the wet stairs to where his wife waited.

"Who were you talking to?" she asked.

"To *you*, of course," he said, a trifle testily. "Why on earth didn't you want me to close the storm windows?"

She stared at him blankly.

"Didn't you yell 'STOP!' a minute ago?" he asked.

Her expression told him all he needed to know.

Several weeks later Lisa was lying in bed, Bob half-dozing beside her, when she began to get a distinct impression of someone reflected in the hallway mirror just outside their door. She nudged Bob who snorted awake.

"Look! Do you see it?"

At first he only saw the reflection of the opposite wall, then it began to seem as though an image was emerging, like layers of paint built up by an artist with his brush.

"What do you see?" asked Lisa.

"I see a young girl...twelve or fourteen, maybe..with long hair."

"Blonde?"

"Yes, light blonde. And her dress..."

"Could be a blouse. Does it look light blue to you?"

Bob shook his head. "That I can't tell. But it does have these sort of wavy frills."

"Ruffles on the front? My God, I see it, too!"

Bob saw the girl as somewhat older than Lisa did; he also did not see the color in her clothing.

Mutual hallucination? Leading questions from Lisa or the suggestibility of the couple? All might be a possibility except that they weren't the first to see the girl in the mirror.

Virginia* told Rod Senter Jr., who grew up in the house across the street, that she and several local ladies were at the house playing bridge with Trudy Prescott, the owner. Virginia decided to have a little fun and said to Trudy, "Have you heard of Priscilla, the little girl ghost who rolls barrel hoops down the stairs at night?"— making up the "ghost" story and the name on the spot, thinking she would spook Trudy.

Trudy looked surprised. "Oh..." she said, "you've seen her *too*?" She described a young, school-age girl with long blonde hair and a 19th-century ankle-length dress.

The Haases never knew Trudy *or* Virginia. Which leads to the puzzling question: how could Virginia "make up" a ghost seen by at least three other people?[1]

SMOKE

Historian Rick Crawford was driving through a valley in southern Logan County at dusk one September evening in 1993. He'd spent the day researching Indian village sites in the area for a book and his mind drifted to the names of former settlements—Pigeon Town, DeGraff, Blue Jacket's Village. All were destroyed in October of 1786 when General Logan swept through the valley, burning Indian settlements.

Drawn back from his daydreaming, Rick suddenly realized that the entire valley floor was covered with a blue mist hanging five to six feet off the ground. Puzzled, he looked for a brush fire, although, as he said later, "I *knew* that a brush fire couldn't cause that much smoke. Maybe a forest fire could, but not just an ordinary brush fire."

Rick was traveling in a very isolated part of Logan County, not a thickly-populated county to begin with. Rick couldn't even see a farmhouse. He rolled down his window and

There was a scent of wood smoke and of food cooking throughout the entire valley. At DeGraff and West Liberty Rick mentioned the smoke to the local residents.

"They sort of smiled and said, 'Oh? You noticed that too?' They told me that it always happened at dusk—that smell of cooking and smoke. And then I remembered that it was the custom of the Shawnee to cook their main meal at dusk."

SENSING SIDNEY

"I moved into the house in Novelty, east of Cleveland, and within two days, I heard the car accident that killed Sidney," said Tom. "It was around three in the afternoon. I was sitting in a chair reading, when I heard the sound of a car smashing into the house. I heard glass break and thought I felt the house shake. It startled me enough that I spilled my soda! I went outside, but there was no sign of any accident. I checked the roof to see if debris had landed on it but nothing was there. After walking all around the property, I concluded that I must have nodded off and dreamed it.

"I heard it two other times in the early hours of the morning. On both occasions, I woke up hearing what I thought was the residual sound of the accident. Finally I asked the real estate agent why the house was being rented. I found out that the former owner, Sidney, was killed in an automobile accident when a drunk driver crossed a yellow line and hit him head-on, killing him instantly."

"I began to sleep on my back with the light on because I kept waking up with the sensation that someone was standing over me. It was enough to scare me awake for hours. As long as I had the light on, I could *see* that no one was there and fall back to sleep. I often heard the back door open and someone large walk into the kitchen and begin talking. I could never understand the words, but I knew it was a man with a deep voice.

"Once as I was watching TV in the living room, I heard the back door open and shut and footsteps entering the kitchen. I thought it was my roommate Chuck. I needed to talk to him, so

I got up and began to walk towards the back door which was visible from the living room. I heard footsteps coming towards me, but it wasn't until the footsteps and I entered opposite sides of the dining room that I realized the steps lacked a body to create them.

"From day one, I felt there was something strange about the basement. In particular, there was this corner area that attracted me every time I went downstairs. There were some shelves littered with old junk. I would go to them and just stand there, feeling like it was an important place at one time. There were times when I would be in the basement and would sense Sidney's energy around me.

"It wasn't until about a year later that I accidentally ran into Sidney's best friend who told me the significance of the corner area. Sidney made violins for a hobby and that area was his workshop. He sometimes spent twelve to fourteen hours a day there making violins.

"Sidney must not have liked my taste in music because my stereo totally stopped working about a month after I moved into the house. I had been turning up the stereo very loud since we were out in the country where we wouldn't bother anyone. When I moved out of the house and into a new apartment, I plugged the stereo in and it has worked fine ever since.

"When the house was put up for sale, Sidney became agitated. He spent all night walking back and forth through the house. Sidney had built the house himself and was obviously distressed by the thought of someone besides himself owning it.

"Sidney found a way to put a damper on the sale. While a realtor and three buyers were looking at the house, Sidney came in the back door. They were standing in the dining room when they heard the back door open and shut, causing them to turn and look toward the kitchen. Sidney apparently walked through the kitchen, through the dining room, (no more than a few feet away) and into the master bedroom. Although they did not see anything, they heard the footsteps. All four looked at each other, said nothing and left the house. The realtor had to take a sabbatical. Last I heard, the house sold, but it took about two years to do so." Maybe Sidney finally met a buyer he liked.

POWERS IN THE ATTIC

Zoar, a postcard-perfect town nine miles south of Canton, was the refuge of the Separatists who had fled religious persecution in Germany. Led by Joseph Bimeler, they arrived in the Tuscarawas Valley in 1817. In 1819, the settlers agreed to pool all their resources in common. Bimeler's charismatic personality and the hard work and devotion of the settlers made Zoar into one of the most successful experiments in communal living ever seen in the United States.

But in 1853 Joseph Bimeler died and the Zoar community began to drift. In 1898, the community sold its communal property, divided the proceeds, and the Society of Separatists was no more. Now the town is on the National Register of Historic Places and many of the old buildings are in private hands.

David is a retired FBI agent. "We aren't supposed to believe in ghosts or spirits," he commented ruefully. "I tried for a long time not to. But there's too much that goes on here.

"The first month and a half, I had trouble sleeping in the house. I kept expecting to see shadows or something else—and hoping that I'd never see them. It preyed on my mind. After six weeks, I just came to grips with it. If there's something here, I thought, it's not evil. This is *your* house. You have a right to live in it, so you'd better start."

David lives in The Boys Dormitory or House Number 17, built in 1828 to house the boys of Zoar, who were taken from their families at age three and required to live in the Dormitory until adulthood. Parents were discouraged from having contact with their children who were instead tended by elderly matrons. The matrons, unfortunately, were sometimes out of sympathy with the children in their care. Thankfully, the concept was done away with in 1860.

The house is a huge wood frame building of 3,400 square feet. There are two floors, plus an attic. Whether seen under snow or behind a white cloud of apple-blossom, the house still has an institutional air, like an inn or barracks. The original plaster walls, oak flooring and woodwork remain, as does a solid walnut staircase ascending three floors. When David moved to the building in January of 1992, his intention was to open the house as a bed and breakfast.

The bed and breakfast has not yet materialized, but the house has been completely renovated, inside and out. An enormous attic runs the width and breadth of the house. When the family first moved in, there were some "rough odors" in the attic. David removed the huge attic wooden floor planks. "I found primitive tools, 1830s coins, toys, marbles—all kinds of things that looked like they had been swept through the cracks." It was like discovering a time capsule.

David's daughter Angela began to attend the local high school. Some of the girls introduced themselves and asked where Angela lived. When they heard she lived in the Boys' Dormitory, they exclaimed, "You don't *sleep* there? Boy, I'd never sleep there anytime. Everybody *knows* that house is haunted!"

Angela brought the story home. Her dad tried to tease her about it, and they all had a good laugh.

"That was the first inkling I had that there might be something unusual about the house," David said. "About a week after we moved into the house, I was down in the cellar, which is a spooky old place. This was very late Saturday night and I assumed that everybody else was sleeping. I had my back turned to the cellar door and was cleaning deposits off the brick floor. I had this strange sensation that someone was watching me. It also sounded like the cellar door had opened. I thought one of the kids was having a good time."

He was so sure, he called out, "Angela, what do you want?"

There was no response.

"I figured she was playing a trick, on account of the stories from school. I immediately went upstairs and checked in her room and my son's room. They were sound asleep. I figured it wouldn't be my wife, but I checked and she too was asleep.

"I went back to the cellar. The same thing happened: the cellar door sounded as if it was opening, kind of a creaking sound. And the feeling of being watched. It gave me cold chills to the point I turned around and faced the door. I said to myself, 'This is ridiculous. You shouldn't worry about this stuff.' I was never one to sleep with the lights on, but now in our very large hallway, we leave on night lights, even when we're asleep."

Five weeks after moving in, David had an experience that he couldn't explain.

"My mother was visiting from Indianapolis. After we were all in bed, I heard the sound of children laughing coming from what seemed to be the attic. I don't know why I didn't get up. I was probably a little startled. Then in the early morning, I was awakened by what sounded like children crying. This time, I did get up. I guess it's that natural parental reaction to check the kids. They were all asleep. I looked outside, but it still sounded like it was coming from the attic."

David took his flashlight and quickly opened the attic door. There was nothing there.

"The next morning, my mother said, 'Did you have children here in the house last night?'

'No, Mom, why?'

'Didn't you hear the children crying?'

'Yeah, I did, Mom,' I said, and laughed nervously. She gave me a look that only a mother can give, wanting an explanation, but knowing she probably wouldn't get one, at least for the time being. A neighbor later told me that the laughing and crying were things that previous tenants had frequently heard.

"I didn't want to scare my mother or get her excited. She has visited since and I have told her I felt the house was haunted. I think she knew all along, though. Now she comes to visit hoping she will experience a haunting again."

About a year and a half after the family moved in, David's son Chris and Steve*, one of his buddies, went up to the attic one night to lift weights. David was on the second floor, reading.

"I heard this scuffle. I heard the attic door open. The next thing I saw what appeared to be a white vapor trail coming out of the attic, down the steps to the second floor, rounding the corner, then heading for the first floor. It was a thin mist, flowing down the steps without any sound. It was about four or five feet long and had a long tail that tapered off at the back. It startled me, but my real concern was with the boys. They were really moving out of that attic! It sounded like a herd of horses.

Steve was as white as a ghost. He said to my son, "Did you see it? Did you see it?"

"Yeah, I saw it," Chris admitted. He was surprised, but not frightened in light of all that had happened in the house. Steve told David how, as he was lifting some weights, he saw a white vapor hovering over him like a cloud. It startled him and he put down the weights and jumped up. The mist shot *under* the door. After a moment's paralysis, the boys went after it.

Steve swore he would never go up into the attic again. And he refuses to stay overnight even today.

"We know that all the boys in Zoar lived in this house; they were required to live here from the age of three by the Trustees. We also know that some of the boys had a difficult time. Some of the Matrons were very stern and strict. I'm guessing that there were some severe beatings when boys misbehaved. I can't substantiate that any boy died in the dorm, but the law of averages would say that some deaths occurred, if nothing else, during the 1830s cholera epidemic."

Of course it's likely that the ghosts are boys, mainly because it was a boys' dorm. The crying and laughing, the jokester types of thing like a rocking chair rocking, doors and windows opening, the lights flickering. They're just having a good time."

And perhaps they're experiencing a normal family life at last.

10

DOOM AT THE INN:
More haunted inns and taverns

Let us eat and drink; for tomorrow we shall die.
-Isaiah 23:13–

THE WOMAN IN BLUE

Cathy Christian called me from her house. She didn't want to talk about the strange spirits at the Olde Trail Tavern in Yellow Springs while she was alone in the place. I can't say that I blame her. The very first time I ever walked into the Tavern, I turned around and walked right out. I thought it was just me; Cathy's story showed me I was wrong. For there's a ghostly woman in blue at the Tavern. No woman has seen her, but they have felt her presence—and they didn't like what they felt.

One of the managers, Walt, was the first to see the ghost.

"It was a weeknight, after dark. I closed up the building, got everybody out and locked the front door. I started counting the money and about ten minutes into it, I heard a noise and saw a woman coming in the front door.

"She was wearing an old-style, blue-and-white print dress. It looked like it was cotton and had a high collar. Her sandy blond hair was pulled up in a bun. She was in her upper 30s, and very attractive. She looked a little different, but, hey, this is Yellow Springs.

"'Excuse me,' I said, 'we're closed; we've been closed for a half-hour.' She smiled, but kept walking. I had money all over the bar so I ignored her for a moment while I finished a count. She walked closer to the bar. I said, 'Excuse me—you'll have to leave!' I said it kind of gruffly, which usually gets a response out of people. I turned to get something to put over the money. I looked in the big mirror behind the bar, but could see nobody behind me even though I could see her by the bar out of the corner of my eye. 'Excuse *me*, we're *closed*,' I said again. She stepped through the archway into the back room."

Walt slammed a pad of paper down on top of the money and ran to go stop her. She was nowhere to be seen.

"I ran upstairs and looked all over the place. I didn't think that much about it, just maybe I was a little loony from the day's work. It kind of blew by me."

The next day Walt started telling Cathy about the woman: "I swear I saw a ghost in here last night, and I don't believe in ghosts."

Before he got into the story or could tell any details, Cathy stopped him. She wanted Walt to talk to someone else first and she brought in Lemoine Rice, a psychic investigator from the Springfield area.

Walt said, "The thing that impressed me was I started the description and before I could spit it out, he finished the description verbatim, using the exact words I had in my mind. That was strange, having somebody giving a description that I was only thinking."

The kitchen manager, Mike, has never seen the lady, but he's seen and heard some *strange* stuff.

"I was standing near the area where the [front and back] buildings connect when, from between the walls, I heard what sounded like a woman talking. I ignored it, thinking someone was upstairs, although only Cathy and me were in the building. I moved away from the wall, then came back. There was definitely something talking between the walls: a muffled woman's voice having a conversation in normal tones. About the same time of day, a couple weeks later, I came in on my morning shift. I was on the stairs and noticed music and conversation upstairs. I thought it was the radio playing and Cathy having friends in. The closer I got, the fainter and fainter the sound got, so by the time I was at the top, it was gone."

Mike gives the ghost a healthy dose of respect: "One time me and the cook were in the kitchen, discussing the possibility of the ghost and laughing about it. Immediately, all the knives and utensils on the magnetic hold-strips came clattering off the strip."

Cathy feels a strange kind of energy on the upper floor.

"It feels like there is a 'beam' [of energy] running from the basement up through the ceiling to the banquet room. I walked through it when I first bought the place and my hair stood on end! The bad feelings are upstairs and the good feelings are downstairs."

A large upstairs room facing Xenia Avenue used to be used as a private party room or for overflow from the downstairs. It was too dark, and too quiet, and dominated by the watchful portraits of a hard-faced pioneer couple. "Nobody ever wanted to sit up there, cut off from the action downstairs. We finally turned it into an office," said Cathy.

It was in her office that Cathy was spooked by an electric piano that sounded like someone was hitting the keys even though it was unplugged. She ran downstairs, then back up with witnesses, who couldn't make it play. Kim Bishop, who wrote an article on the ghost for a Springfield paper said her camera wouldn't work upstairs: "My trusty 35mm struggled desperately in the upstairs room. Down in the bar area, click and whir...it worked perfectly. Back upstairs it whined and groaned as if someone or something was pulling backward on the wind mechanism."[1]

The women's restroom is also upstairs and it was in the dark hallway by the restroom that Fred* the cook saw a woman with long black hair wearing a long, dark dress. Her head was down; her hands were folded in front of her and although her face was in shadow, she looked very sad. Fred assumed it was Teresa, a co-worker.

Downstairs he grumbled to Cathy's father, Roger, "What's wrong with Teresa? She won't speak to me."

"She's not here," Roger said, "She's in Michigan on vacation." "No, she's not. She's standing right up in front of the lady's restroom."

Roger and Fred both went upstairs. The lights were on, but nobody was there. Later Cathy asked Fred, "Did you see her face?"

"No," he said, "her head was down. I thought, 'Is she mad at me?'" "It's probably the ghost," said Cathy. Fred flipped out.

Cathy said, "I made fun of her one night. I was in the bathroom and when two of my friends came in, I stood on the toilet so they wouldn't see my feet. Then I threw open the door and said, 'Boo!' It scared both of them to death.

"The next day everything that was in the cooler froze. The milk, even the heads of cabbage, froze solid. I had to throw away so much food it was ridiculous. The repairman said there was nothing wrong with the equipment. It's like the ghost has some strange energy source. This is why I didn't want to talk about her down there. She freezes me out! I won't ever make fun of her again!

Lemoine Rice said she likes me and what I've done with the place. He knew what I'd said to her about, 'If you're here, and you're protecting the place, that's fine, but I do not want to ever see you.' Lemoine repeated this back to me, word for word. I told him, 'I don't know who scares me more, you or her!'

So what is it about the Tavern's history that could account for the woman in blue?

The Tavern was built in 1827 by Frances Hafner as a stagecoach stop on the Columbus-Cincinnati route. It may be the oldest house in the area. In doing some geneaological research, Mike came across a story: It seems that the Tavern was once a bakery, run by a man and his wife—who was having an affair with the postmaster, whose office stood just across the street. One of the men—we don't know which one— was found dead in front of the tavern with an icepick in his eye.

If the woman in blue was the baker's wife, it raises a haunting question: is she mourning her lost lover or atoning for her guilt?

SPIRITOUS LIQUORS

The Kalida restaurant where Nora worked for nearly two decades was famous throughout northwestern Ohio for great steaks. Its ghosts were an unadvertised special.

The two-story brick building occupied by The Grill Room* was built around 1900. There were nine dining rooms, a large private room for parties, the kitchen, and storage rooms. At the heart of the restaurant was the plush cocktail lounge which opened on the foyer.

One night, the restaurant had been very busy with groups of couples and several large parties. When midnight rolled around, there were still a few patrons lingering over their coffee. Nora, who lived nearby, told the other waitresses to go on home—she would tend to the stragglers. It was 1:00 a.m. before the last customer left. With a sigh of relief, Nora walked around the restaurant, snuffing candles, turning off the coffee pots, and tidying up. Then she walked back to the storage area to say goodnight to the chef who was the only other person left in the building. He assured Nora that he would lock the front door behind her and she made her way to the employee cloak room next to the cocktail lounge.

As Nora slipped into her coat, thinking longingly of a hot shower and a soft bed, she froze. Coming from the cocktail lounge was the sound of laughter, of glasses tinkling, of ice against glass, and many people talking. Nora was appalled. The party sounded like it was in full swing and the prospect of being stuck there for another hour or two, serving drinks and coffee while the party wound down was not appealing!

Sighing, she hung up her coat, pasted on a smile, and pushed through the swinging doors to the lounge. Instantly, all the sounds from the cocktail lounge stopped, as if they had been switched off, like you'd turn off a TV. Even in the dim light of the lounge, Nora could see that there wasn't a soul there. Only seconds before, she had heard the sounds of merrymaking, now all was deathly still.

Nora just stood there, shocked, then slowly turned and gazed around the room. There was a strange feeling in the air, as if unseen eyes were staring at her, as if she had crashed a party where she was not welcome. It was not a comfortable feeling. "What in the *world*...?" she thought. "This shouldn't be; this isn't natural."

Nora was so startled, she went back to the kitchen to see if the chef had a radio on. He didn't and was just getting ready to leave. "I just thought I heard a party in the cocktail lounge," she told him. He shrugged it off. Nora told only her family and a few friends. She didn't want to get a reputation as a nut.

Nora doesn't know of any deaths in the building. However, she did note that the incident happened a few months after the sudden death of the restaurant's owner. He had devoted his whole life to building up the business from a one-room eatery to an entire building. Nora says he loved to entertain people; had a real gift for it. Perhaps he just invited a few, very old friends over—after hours.

CURIOUS GHOST

The October day was raw and overcast with a wind that whipped up my skirts as well as the leaves. "Thank God for petticoats," I thought, lugging my suitcase up the stairs of the elegant Victorian house. I rang the bell and tried to peer through the multiple panes of beveled glass that reminded me of a bee's multi-lensed eyes.

The door was opened, not by a maid in black uniform and white collar and cuffs, but by a young woman in jeans and a sweatshirt. She is Janet Rogers, the owner of Medina's Spitzer House Bed & Breakfast, built in 1890 by banker Ceilan Milo Spitzer.

The hall and stairway were richly lined with cherry paneling. I glimpsed a portiere-framed door leading to an elegant dark parlor with a piano swathed in a shawl and decorated with a cluster of silver-framed family portraits.

"We're not really busy in the middle of the week so you'll have your choice of rooms," Janet told me, leading the way up the stairs.

"Just give me something warm," I shivered.

"This is the warmest," she said, unlocking the door and switching on the light. "This is Ceilan's Room."

I stepped into the room and immediately stepped backwards. The light went out; so did the ones in the hall. All the lights in the house had gone off at that moment. A headless mannequin stood in the bedroom, dressed in a cream-colored, late-1800s wedding dress. The room felt freezing to me and I sensed an unseen male presence. Janet clicked the light switch. Nothing happened.

"Does that happen often in that room?" I asked.

"No," Janet said and she seemed embarrassed.

"Let's see what else you have," I said, politely.

She unlocked a door at the top of the stairs. "This is Anna's Room. It isn't so warm since it's at the front of the house, but it does have an electric space heater."

I breathed a sign of relief. Although a rather unnerving white embroidered nightgown was hung on the back of the bathroom door (I made a mental note to take it down at bedtime, so I didn't meet it in the dark) the room was quite comfortable with rosy wallpaper, oak furniture, and plump pillows.

I ironed my blouse for the evening's event at the haunted Hinkley Library and went out to give my talk. When I returned, I was tired but keyed-up, as I usually am after chatting for several hours. I took a hot shower in the deep, old-fashioned tub. While groping for shampoo from the basket of toiletries Janet had thoughtfully provided, I had a sudden weird impression that something was about to put the shampoo bottle helpfully into my hand.

I put the thought out of my mind as I climbed out of the shower, wrapped myself in a towel, and opened the bathroom door to let out the steam. A young woman was standing there.

She was a short, stout woman, in her twenties, perhaps, wearing what could have been a striped skirt and waist or what the Edwardians called a "wrapper" or housedress. She also wore a long apron tied around her thick waist. I could tell her smooth hair was parted in the middle, but I wasn't getting much facial detail other than a heavy jaw.

"Are you pregnant?" she asked me in a curiously nasal tone. Without thinking, I replied, "No, just fat."

"How old are you? Do you have any children? What are you doing here?" The questions came in rapid fire, without waiting for my replies. I stammered answers, more than a little dazed by this chattering apparition. Studying her, I realized she was what might have been called "simple" or "not quite right." In the nineteenth century, such family members were often regarded as an embarrassment and locked away in attics and institutions. She was very nosy and completely unself-conscious. Then, just as suddenly, apparently losing interest, she was gone.

I brushed my hair and teeth, took down the antique nightgown and laid it on the rocking chair and went to bed with a book. About 11:00 p.m. I heard the tinny, clashing sound of the piano in the parlor downstairs. Two chords were played once, then once again. I had a feeling that this wasn't Janet dusting the keys. I was a bit nervous that the nosy girl might come back and wake me up, but drifted off easily enough—with the light on and the book still on my lap.

"WHAM!" I was awakened by a sudden violent blow on the bathroom door , which was close by my bed.

I smiled and thought, "OK, whoever you are, goodnight." I turned off the light and slept peacefully until morning.

Coming out of my room for breakfast, I saw the girl standing at the very end of the long hall that led to the servant's stair to the kitchen. She looked vaguely in my direction. That was all. I couldn't tell if the girl was a servant, although her clothes might indicate she was, or a daughter of the house. Ceilan and his wife Lillian had no children—that we know about. It would have been intensely mortifying for a man labeled the "genius" of his family to have sired a less-than-perfect child. Adequate reason to conceal such a child, if that were the case.

I was lavishly breakfasted in the cheerful dining room that was full of cookie jars and 1950s collectible glassware. I told Janet about the ghost and not only was she intrigued, but she had her own stories to tell.

When Janet bought the house, she was working a regular full-time job with fifteen-hour days. "I worked so much, I never paid attention to anything here. But when I worked at the house all the time, I started hearing things. When we first moved in, there were light fixtures in the basement that turned on with a pull string. I couldn't reach any of them until my husband put longer strings on them. I went down in the basement once and none of the lights would work. I discovered the bulbs had been twisted so far, that they were broken off in the sockets. My husband thought I'd done it, but why would I? I couldn't even reach them.

"Then there was the time I heard two gentlemen talking in the dining room. My bedroom is just off the dining room and I thought my husband had come home and was talking to someone, that's how distinct it was. I didn't get up because I didn't want to get dressed. But I kept thinking, 'When is he going to get done?' Finally I didn't hear the voices anymore and I went out to look. My husband was not home.

"I'll be lying in my bed watching TV when I'll hear heels, like a woman's footsteps clicking on the floor just above my room. I go upstairs, thinking it's my daughter. I yell for her and she doesn't answer. So I'll open the front door; there's nobody in the driveway. I go *that* far, thinking it's a real person. I never think first that it's a ghost.

"My daughter used to sleep in Anna's Room. She would always feel like somebody was in the room with her. She'll still tell you that today. She would hear a girl's voice—a very noisy girl—at night."

Janet has also had guests ask her about a noisy girl in the upstairs hall. "One morning a guest told me, 'What was your daughter laughing at last evening? Boy, she was really laughing out there in the hall last night!" I had to tell her that my daughter wasn't home. The guest didn't buy it.

'Well, there was a young lady in the hall giggling and laughing up a storm for most of the evening. Do you have ghosts?' the guest demanded.

Janet was cautious, "Well, I've had guests *tell* me that I do...."

"Another guest wandered down the back staircase into the kitchen and felt like someone was following him closely. *He* also asked if we had ghosts."

After breakfast, I signed the guestbook in the parlor. Then I strolled over to the piano and lifted the lid. It had been closed the afternoon before, when I arrived, and I got the impression that the instrument wasn't played very often. After a few out-of-tune chords, I knew why. The chords I'd heard so late at night had a tentative sound, like a child fingering the keys, trying out notes. I wondered if it had been the curious ghost.

About a year ago, Janet put a bell on the front door; someone has been coming and going ever since. Janet hears it ring and thinks, "I don't have a guest tonight." But when she checks the door it's always locked. And Janet knows who her guest is.

THIS IS THE SONG THAT NEVER ENDS

The Baird House of Ripley has seen a lot of history sweeping up and down the Ohio River. It was occupied for 125 years by the Baird family. It has nine Italian marble fireplaces, an enormous French crystal chandelier, and at least one ghost. Its straightforward red brick facade, built in 1825, was, in a later, more frivolous era, trimmed with lacy wrought iron brought by packet boat from Cincinnati. The effect is charmingly toy-like, as if it belongs under a glass bell, arranged in a cork and wax-flower landscape, on a Victorian parlor mantelpiece.

Ripley, known for the Rankin House, where runaway slaves crossing the Ohio River could see a light shining in the

window, was a house divided. Many in town were abolition-
ists, with secret tunnels and rooms in their homes. Others
would have been just as happy to capture the escaping slaves
and return them to their masters. Just eight miles down the
river, in Kentucky, the city of Augusta was attacked on
September 28, 1862, terrifying Judith Liggett Baird, who could
see the smoke from Front Street in Ripley.

Patricia and Glenn Kittles, who now run the Baird House
Bed & Breakfast, have a copy of Judith Baird's letter to her
husband, Major Chambers Baird, who was a paymaster
stationed in Washington DC.

"I'd just discovered it in a local history book and I was
reading the letter in the parlor," said Glenn. "We had some
guests sitting in there at the same time. A lamp in the corner
kept flickering. My wife looked at it; her eyebrows went up. I
kept on reading. The light kept on flickering. My wife got on
her hands and knees to check the plug. Before she could touch
the plug, the light went out, then came back on and blinked and
flickered. We checked the bulb and it was fine. The couple
with us stared with eyes as big as saucers! I've read the letter
several times since then, but the light hasn't flickered again."

The Kittles think that Judith Baird might haunt the house.

"We also fantasize about Florence," said Glenn. "Florence
Baird was an opera star who sang with the New York Metro-
politan Opera. She was the last of the Baird family and died in
1973.

"When we first moved here, Patricia heard somebody
warming up—like an opera singer—in the upstairs hallway,
you know, 'ha, ha, ha, ha, ha' up and down the scale. We
believe it was Florence."

A lot of the strange happenings are noises. Pat hears men
creeping upstairs. She's heard people humming upstairs or
sounds like a radio that can't be pinpointed. Sometimes when
Pat or Glenn is playing tunes on the organ, it shuts itself off,
but only during wild raucous music. Apparently Florence has
refined musical tastes!

"We also have a big gray ghost cat. You'll see it flash by out of the corner of your eye, then it's gone. Or you'll feel something swish past you in the hallway, just a wisp. It doesn't make any noise."

"No, we don't have a real cat," Glenn told me, "Pat says the only good cat's a dead one." So that's the kind they have.

Another possible ghostly inhabitant is Harold Baird, Florence's brother. He was an aviator in the First World War and the first to do the barrel-roll acrobatic maneuver.

"He was also an alcoholic," said Glenn. "When he was inebriated, he'd pull the car up into the backyard, almost onto the porch, and sleep it off in the car. I hope he doesn't come after me for telling you this!"

"Every night we shut the big front door and lock it around 9:30 or 10:00 p.m. with a key that looks like it's half a foot long. Invariably, within a half hour, we hear that door open and shut and I say, 'There's Harold.' One time I said, 'Hi, Harold!' and scared Pat half to death.

"I've been upstairs and I felt like somebody tapped me on the shoulder. I turned and nobody was there. I tried to attribute it to a jumpy muscle.

"We've seen a picture of the house when there was a canopy bed in the corner in the fourth floor bedroom. That bed is now in our Ripley museum. We built a small closet into that corner and we'd always find the hangers on the floor. You could pick them up and hang them on the rack, then close the door and you'd hear, 'Crash! Bang! Bang!' and the hangers would be back on the floor again. Pat also heard her hat and shoe boxes rattling something awful. She thought all the boxes had fallen off the shelves, but everything was in place when she opened the closet. We began to wonder if somebody had died in that corner in the bed. We found that everything would be OK if we kept the closet door open. So we don't close it any more.

"When we first came here, we chose colors for our parlor walls and carpet. The walls were painted two colors of a hideous blue. Just 'out of the blue,' we decided on soft yellow walls with a white border and a hunter green carpet."

Later, the couple went to Williamsburg where they found that the yellow they had selected was called Chamber's Palace Yellow, and the green was called Chambers Palace Green. Two of the Baird men were named Chambers. In addition, they discovered that the fabric they chose for the parlor was called Florence Midnight.

"We feel we were destined to have this place," Glenn told me. "When we first pulled up in front and saw four music lyres in the wrought iron that runs across the whole front of the house, I knew we had to buy the place. I've been a professional musician since 1941. We feel that these things brought us together. I guess we're crazy!

"But whatever is here, it's friendly and seems happy about what we're doing here. The Bairds lived here for three generations over 125 years. We are the 11th owners in 172 years. I hope we can keep it in the family."

NIGHTMARE ON MAIN STREET

When I first saw the Piqua hotel, I thought of the description in Shirley Jackson's *The Haunting of Hill House*: "This house...reared its great head back against the sky without concession to humanity. It was a house without kindness, never meant to be lived in, not a fit place for people or for love or for hope." It was huge—a massive beast crouching on a typical midwestern main street. There were turrets and balconies, and a tower where only a ghostly shadow remained of a clock's face.

Much of the facade was encrusted with a crawling fretwork of saw-toothed vines with sinister little faces peeping out from the foliage. There was an African-American head and a Native American head and some faces that looked very much like Green Men, the monstrous carvings found on Romanesque churches.

Several carved heads, nearly life-size, and high on the tower, caught my eye. One seemed to be half-man, half-grinning tusked walrus. Another had a flat, flayed face, like a skinned corpse with something ancient and watchful about its drilled eyes.

In the dusty tiled foyer, I met Martha Hardcastle-Guthrie, who had worked for several years to get me into the building. Accompanying her were her friends, historian Jim Oda, Valryn Bush, Kiersten Knore, and Lisa Perry.

I swallowed hard the minute I walked in the door. The massive lobby was gloomy and cavernous. This time, instead of a blow to the stomach, I got a one-two punch. The energy in the lobby was palpable. I wandered, taking in the sweeping marble staircase, an enormous gilt pier mirror speckled with age, a hooded fireplace huge enough for a chateau. It looked like a set from *Citizen Kane*.

Jim led the way to the basement. Paint chips, plaster and lathe crunched underfoot. I gasped as I got to the bottom of the stairs. Even surrounded by this many people, I was utterly terrified. Of what, I couldn't say. All I could do was keep walking, hoping blindly that there would be an end, that we would go back up those stairs to the daylight.

The only light came from Jim's flashlight. He directed it first at a men's lavatory, filled with disemboweled toilets and unnameable droppings. The flashlight's beam barely penetrated into the next few rooms, all apparently storage rooms, all dark, all debris-filled and all nerve-wracking.

Cautioning us about a low arch and an incline, Jim took us into the boiler room where I was startled by the bright, artificial glow of a neon light. I thought I would never find my way out of that darkness. Jim pointed out the old boiler whose door stood open. I had a brief flash of a young African-American man sweating as he shoveled coal into it.

After one more subterranean room filled with old machinery, we emerged into the lobby once more. I stared upwards at the painted-over skylight, the peeling, coffered ceiling and the carved railing surrounding the mezzanine. Jim told us this was the ladies' lobby area, reached by their own private stair.

And on that mezzanine was a lady. She wore a dark dress with the extremely wide, leg-o-mutton sleeves of 1895-97 that made women look like butterflies. Her hair was dressed high and close to her head. She wore a tiny hat with a spray of skeletal black egret feathers. I began to shake when I saw her.

As I climbed the sweeping divided staircase to the mezzanine, I examined the arched stained glass window in warm shades of gold and yellow glass. Pressboard showed through gaping holes in the glass. At the very top, the leading was twisted violently inward, as if something had exploded through it. Val snapped a picture of the window.

I paused on the landing and leaned on the newel post, too exhausted to go on. Automatically I scribbled notes, my hand shaking badly. At the top of the stairs, I turned a corner into a hallway that led to the guest rooms.

"Where is he? Where is he? Where is he?" The words came, obsessive and terrifying.

I was trembling and began to limp. The woman in black was searching for someone: a lover, a seducer, a cad, who never came. Mentally I said, "He's not here, he's not coming, he'll never come."

"Where is he? Where is he? Where is he?" The words beat against my ears like moths battering against a screen. They didn't stop until I was in the opposite wing.

In a row of decaying rooms, I walked into a closet where a man had hanged himself. Looking at the relatively modern clothes rods, logic took over. He couldn't have hung himself from *these* rods. Oh, you're *always* seeing hanged people... I chided myself, and moved on.

The corner suite on the mezzanine was a relatively cheerful room with plenty of light, a fireplace with a tile surround, and peeling wallpaper. In the rounded tower portion stood a big man, legs braced apart, exuding energy and confidence. He was a man of substance, heavily involved in politics. He wore a Prince Albert frock coat, and an immaculately white high, stiff collar with a stick-pinned tie. He reminded me a bit of Teddy Roosevelt or perhaps William Howard Taft—someone of that generation.

I darted in and out of rooms that had obviously been lived in sometime in the last ten years. Martha and the other women whispered like mice in the hall behind me. I brooded on the woman on the mezzanine. I was getting the image of a woman confronting her betrayer, an image of shooting in the lobby, at the bottom of the stairs.

"Too much like a stage melodrama," I scoffed to myself, "The Wronged Woman shooting the Cad with her dainty pearl-handled gun!"

At the very end of the hall, in a room where the tattered rose-print wallpaper hung like moire ribbons, the words returned, but they were my own, "Where are you? Where are you?"

"Right behind you," came the answer.

I found myself facing a blurry wall mirror. Nothing reflected beside my own face.

The speaker was a young man about town, the very type who would have jilted the woman on the mezzanine—only he was about a decade too late. His smart suit had the tight fit and high-waisted jacket of 1915-17. He was what might have been called a "nut," a young lothario who would have smoked, drank, gambled, and vigorously sowed his wild oats wherever he could. He was smooth-faced and vicious and I didn't like him one bit.

I turned down another corridor. He followed me, smirking, as if he could read my thoughts about his morals.

"You jerk," I said angrily, "You..."— at that point I got rather nasty with him. His well-bred vulgarity seemed to bring out the worst in me.

"Such language from a lady!" he said lightly, and disappeared.

After Jim's assurance that the upper floors were safe, I climbed the debris-littered stairs to the third floor. The higher up we went, the worse shape the rooms were in. Ceilings had collapsed in a mess of plaster, lathe, and animal droppings. A trapped pigeon hurled itself against a window. A spidery skeleton splayed in a nest of sodden feathers, like an archaeopteryx fossil, showed that many birds had found their way in but not out again. Much as I love historic buildings, I couldn't imagine trying to restore this tragically decayed structure.

I stopped shaking by the third floor, away from the lady searching obsessively for her lover. Although we had to step around a decaying pigeon on the red-carpeted stairs, the fourth floor was better still. There I found the kitchens (with a memory of a rather profane cook), a startling lime-green dining room and a cooler area with four iron-bound doors open in a row, like doors in a crypt.

The last stairway was steep and forbiddingly narrow. The fifth floor had been the staff rooms. The walls of the airless little cells were soaked in misery. I imagined rising at 5 or 6 a.m. in a room with no electricity, no plumbing and no heat. I imagined scurrying along the narrow hall to the sink by the landing to fill my wash jug with icy water.

The room at the end of the hall was set in a little square corner tower. I edged through the tiny diagonal hall and peeked around the corner. There, propped up against the wall in a sitting position was a dead man. He was middle-aged, nearly bald, with a fringe of hair over his ears, wearing a white shirt with a band-collar. His hands rested stiffly on his thighs. I got the impression of a waiter at the hotel, who, feeling faint, had just slid down the wall and died. I ducked back into the hall.

I had had enough. After a quick glance around the clock tower, I wobbled down the steps to the oppressive fifth floor, then down the red-carpeted stairs, stepping carefully over the dead pigeon.

Back in the tiled foyer, Jim filled us in with some historical background. The hotel was built by William P. Orr and Samuel K. Statler in 1890-91 as the Plaza. It was remodeled in 1914 by Stanhope Boal who dubbed it The Favorite Hotel after his Favorite Stove and Range Company. It was later renamed the Hotel Fort Piqua, the name it bears today.

Why was such a massive hotel built in Piqua? I asked Jim. He smiled.

"Troy had just built their new courthouse and Piqua wanted to have a grand new building too. By an amazing coincidence, the architect of the Troy courthouse, J. W. Yost, designed the Plaza. There has always been a great rivalry between Piqua and Troy."

The hotel was often visited by politicians and presidents, who spoke from the balcony over the main door. Orr and Statler were staunch Republicans. Teddy Roosevelt, William Howard Taft, and Warren Harding all spoke from the balcony with its spiral ironwork railing.

The hotel had the first bar to open in Piqua after Prohibition was repealed in 1933. In 1947-8, African-Americans sat down at the hotel's lunch counter, beginning desegregation in the community. Piqua's only bookie had a betting parlour in the hotel in the 1920s and 30s. It had its own electrical generator because the city's electric plant shut down at dusk. It brought the first sewer system to Piqua.

Like most hotels, the Hotel Fort Piqua had its tragedies. A man digging a trench for the sewer system was buried alive. A workman standing on a barrel of acid used to clean pipes fell through the lid and was terribly hurt. A porter moving a salesman's trunks on a dolly was crushed when they fell on him. A mysterious skeleton was found when the basement was excavated in 1890. A police officer and a criminal shot each other to death in the lobby in 1970. Only one suicide—a hanging—was associated with the hotel and the newspaper report did not give the room number so I could not verify the hanged man I felt.

In 1984, the last hotel guests turned in their keys. After that, the building served as low-income/transient housing. The last living residents moved out in 1987. Since then it has bounced from owner to owner, all with schemes to bring back the hotel's glory days. There are currently plans to turn it into a 70-room hotel and restaurant.

Afterwards we went around the corner to a sports bar to relax with cold drinks. I read off my notes about the ghosts and memories I had seen. At my description of the big man in the corner turret room, Jim said instantly, "That was Stanhope Boal. He weighed in at around 350 pounds. That corner room was his sister's suite." He also told me about Roosevelt and Taft visiting.

I have no idea why the young man haunts the hotel. Revisiting the scene of his indiscretions perhaps? I don't know why I did not sense the police shooting in the lobby or the porter being crushed by the elevator on the third floor. I sensed a shooting, but I thought it was on or near the grand stairs and from the 1890s. Perhaps I am more in tune with that time period.

I shudder when I think of the pitiful woman on the mezzanine. She is so wrapped in her misery, so focused on her own suffering that she can't realize that it is time to move on—to get an after-life, to use Jim's phrase. I can sympathize, but her self-centered sorrow is keeping her prisoner.

I was happy to be out of the hotel. Outside, Martha, Val and I picked out the various nasty carvings on the limestone facade.

"They're worse when you see them through a telephoto lens," Val assured us. I believed her.

I saw some of Val's photos later. She had been snapping pictures throughout the inside of the hotel, but only a few of them turned out. The faces on the outside, however, were crystal clear; I think I was relieved that none of the photos showed anything extra.

Perhaps one day the Hotel Fort Piqua will come alive again with the sound of a jazz band, the tinkle of crystal, the bubble of champagne. Perhaps the sun will glitter once more through the stained glass on the polished marble stairs. Perhaps—one day—the lobby will be thronged with the living instead of the dead...

11

A SEANCE OF SPOOKS:
Multiple hauntings

There must be ghosts all over the world.
-Henrik Ibsen-

Some sites are haunted by more than one ghost or manifestation. However, only rarely do multiple ghosts seem to interact with each other. Even in the most crowded haunted houses, the ghosts must be very lonely.

THE HOUSE OF THE SPIRITS

It had rained and the day was overcast. As I drove the country road near Troy, I could see a house across the fields. It was a square, ugly house sided with what looked like dirty brick paper. It looked cold and abandoned. My heart sank as I saw the address on the mailbox, realizing that this was the house I was supposed to visit.

The owner would probably have a rusting car up on blocks, and a dead tractor graveyard out back, I grumbled to myself. The car slowly crunched up the long sandy drive. I noticed a deep stream, almost a canal, on my right where a shaggy blue heron stood motionless in the shallows. On its bank, a sinister folk-art scarecrow leaned to one side.

Yet, as I pulled into the graveled parking area, I saw that the house was different. Its brick seemed freshly sandblasted. Little electric candles twinkled in all the windows, a colorful banner hung from the eaves, wicker furniture with flowered cushions stood on the porch. The house was tightly contained within a fence. Flowers and herbs ran riot among cement statues of rabbits. Inside, the floors were freshly sanded; the walls whitewashed and stenciled.

I shook hands with Rob and Kathy, who bought the house in October of 1992. They stood outside on the porch while I prowled the house, which was dark even for an overcast day. Almost immediately I felt someone watching me.

I started to go into the narrow parlor that ran along the side of the house beyond the stairs, but something hit me in the stomach as I entered the room. I decided to save the parlor until last. A silvery mercury-glass witch-ball on the table winked at me as I retreated. I pretended to look around the living room then turned to face my watcher.

Standing in the door of the parlor was a lovely young girl. She wore an ankle-length full-skirted dress of dull black taffeta. The dress had long tight sleeves and had nothing, not even a white collar, to relieve its severity. The girl was very young— 13 or 14. Her dark hair was parted in the middle. I got the distinct impression that this was her first long, grown-up dress and she was quite proud of it. At this time young girls wore short dresses until they reached their teens. She seemed friendly, but I still decided to save the room for last.

In the kitchen, I felt silly when I was startled by a tall bunny broom cover of almost-human height. Down in the basement, I got the image of a knot of terror-stricken children hunched, looking up at the ceiling above, as if hearing footsteps approaching. It was like a memory recorded on the site, rather than a true ghost and I could not tell anything else about the children. Rob later told me there was a possibility that the house had been a stop on the Underground Railroad.

Next I went into a bathroom beyond the kitchen and behind the little parlor. As I looked into the mirror, I kept thinking something would reflect back in that other room. I nearly dashed through the parlor, past the antique sofa, piano, and keyboard on my way to the upstairs. I trudged up the steep stairs to the second-floor hall. I felt like I should be very quiet to avoid attracting the attention of the presences in the house.

I glanced into the bathroom, then reluctantly entered it. It was very large and had obviously been carved out of a bedroom. Usually homes of this era had no indoor bathrooms. Kathy had tried her best to make the room inviting. There were scented soaps, candles, and plants. And a coffin on sawhorses by the window. Strangely, I saw two different occupants in the coffin, one after the other. Or perhaps it was just that this was where the household dead were laid out and I was seeing two separate dead men. One was a youngish man in a blue Union uniform. The other was an older man with a hooked nose and short goatee like pictures of Uncle Sam.

Next I glanced in at the master bedroom, which, to my relief, was empty of anything supernatural. I went back out into the narrow hall, hung with an antique quilt. In front of the window stood a middle-aged woman. Her back was turned to me. She wore a dark dress of the Civil War era. She stared fixedly out the window, her arms clutched across her middle, elbows rigid, shoulders hunched. I got the feeling of someone pacing with worry and impatience. Had she been waiting an eternity for the young man who came back in a coffin?

I edged by her into Rob's office. Then I went back downstairs and outside to find the couple. "All done," I said, with a brightness I didn't feel.

"Did you go upstairs into the attic?" Rob asked.

"Um, no," I said, flustered. "There was a potted plant in front of the door." A dead giveaway that something needed to be kept out of—or in—the attic.

"Oh, you've got to see the attic," he said, and went upstairs to move the plant out of the way so I could pass. I climbed the ladder-steep stairs into a place distractingly filled with negative energy, almost like static interference on a radio.

The attic was a place of dark wood and nail-ends. One of the upright posts held the memory of someone tied to it, beaten by a leather strap or belt. I felt the presence of a cruel-hearted man who had hung himself somewhere in the attic. I kept studying the roof and the beams, muttering obsessively, "How did you do it? How could you do it?" I could almost hear him chuckling meanly over my perplexity at the puzzle.

As I turned and picked my way down the dangerously steep stairs, I figured it out and began to chuckle rather meanly myself:

"So *that's* how you did it," I said. The suicide had somehow fastened the noose to the top of the stairwell and swung down the stairs. I hung onto the bannister with extra care; I wouldn't care to spend *my* eternity haunting the house with this unpleasant character. His influence seemed to pervade the entire house.

We all sat in down in the living room to chat. Kathy struck me as a kind-hearted, generous, normally happy woman, but she was edgy. "She's usually a-bubble all the time," said Rob. "but this house has taken it out of her."

As I talked to Kathy, the young girl stood in the door of parlor, watching. I kept one eye on her as we talked.

"She's very pretty," I said to Kathy. "She's smiling now. She likes it that I said she's pretty."

When I got to the coffin in the bathroom, Kathy drew in her breath: "I just want to cry every time I go into that bathroom," she said. "There's this terrible feeling of sadness.

"It's true," said Rob, "She comes out crying and when I ask her why she's crying, she says, 'I don't know.' She never stays in there long. I can't relax and soak in the tub either.

"I always think of death when I go in there," Kathy said. "We found the initials 'K.T.' etched into a pane in a window by the tub. Somehow we overlooked it; we didn't see it when we washed the windows. In fact, we first noticed the initials two whole years after moving in."

As I was talking things over with the couple, I complimented them on a lovely country home.

"You should have seen this place when we bought it," said Rob. "It was the worst dump you've ever seen! The renters left it really trashy."

At that, I told them what I'd seen over the fields: the dingy brick, the darkened windows.

Kathy gave a knowing smile when I mentioned not seeing any candles. She was coming home one day and saw that, on the second floor, all the candles were out. She thought, 'Now, wait a minute...' Then she got up closer to the house, they were back on.

"I was super uncomfortable after we moved in," Rob said. "I couldn't relax. There was just a strange sort of energy in the house. Something still blows out the lightbulbs. We have to replace them constantly. I've replaced the bulb in the same light three times in one week. And the energy fluctuates in waves in this house. There are weeks when I'm real comfortable and I think, 'If this house could stay this way, I wouldn't want to leave.' The next week, the house gets very uncomfortable."

"I told my wife that something here liked us restoring the house. It was like someone looking over my shoulder as I was slaving away at night, saying, 'Man, you're doing a great job!' Everything was A-OK until the night we moved in. Then things went sour."

Three weeks after they moved in, they had closed the door at the bottom of the stairs to keep the dogs out of the upstairs. Rob had gone to work. Then Kathy came downstairs and shut the door. When she came back from work, she opened the door and found the stair runner on the other side ripped to shreds.

"I was so concerned I brought a friend over, handed him a piece of the carpet, and said, 'Try to tear this apart,'" Rob said. "There was no way! I replaced it—and it happened again a week later! It happened a total of three times in three months. "I think it was a kind of test—they were trying to scare us, to see if we'd perservere. We've found if we leave the door open, it doesn't happen."

As I sat there, talking to the couple, I got an impression that the watching woman from upstairs had come into the parlor. She was very severe, of a very conservative religious group, something like Pennsylvania Dutch German or Dutch Brethren.

"Do you have any trouble with Christmas decorations?" I asked, out of the blue.

"I love decorating," Kathy said. "But I can hardly decorate at Christmas—I feel so depressed; like something is holding me back."

Rob added, "I love writing Christmas cards; I always write personal or funny messages. I couldn't even write a Christmas card. I couldn't do it at home. I took them to work and wrote them. There with no problem, but at home I couldn't fill out one Christmas card! Like I said, I can't relax here. You always have to be doing something. The only time you can relax is if you go outside."

I wondered if this was the older woman's influence. I could almost hear her say, "Idle hands are the Devil's playground..."

Kathy put in, "I used to play the piano and keyboard, but now I feel uncomfortable playing music in that room. I feel like I'm just not supposed to play."

Although realizing that the atmosphere in the house is not a good one, Rob tries to keep a positive attitude.

"Since you told us about the girl in the music room," he told me later, "I'll say 'How ya doing, Sarah?' when I pass there. It seems to fit and I thought she might like it and it might make the room more comfortable. We'll hear noises coming out of there while we're watching TV. The silver tea set starts to rattle. The dogs avoid that room. Upstairs, I'll turn that corner and I get super cold, like running into somebody. I just say to myself, 'Get out of my way!'

"Some nights I'll hear the desk drawers in my office going in and out—clunk, clunk. When I go into the office, there's nothing going on. I'll get back in bed; here it goes again. 'Kathy,' I say, 'just turn up the TV.'

Although hauntings rarely come to this, I suggested to Kathy and Rob that they might want to think about moving. The lines between Kathy's eyes showed the strain she was under. They were a young couple and I shuddered to think of bringing a child into that house. The rigid woman upstairs and the mean-hearted suicide from the attic were producing an atmosphere that was not conducive to a tranquil family life.

Rob admitted that they did not want to stay in the house. "We had this house on the market for about four months. We put a contract on another house but it fell through. We're considering building on the property. The views are so nice. I'd just leave this house empty. If they want it, they can have it. The property is so beautiful and the house is so dark..." he said with regret.

Terrified children in the cellar, a lovely young girl in the parlor, a harsh and anxious woman pacing the upper hall, a coffin in the bathroom, and a suicide in the attic. A full—and fearful—house, indeed.

THE BLUE COAT BOY

The stark brick building on the hilltop near Lebanon looked like an orphanage straight out of Dickens. Anne, Rosi, and I shuddered looking at it, even in the bright sunshine.

The Orphans' Asylum and Children's Home, as it was called for over 100 years, was built in 1874, the result of a bequest from Miss Mary Ann Klingling. Prevented by her parents from marrying the man she loved, she was sent to America where she never wed. Perhaps inspired by her lover, who died young and left his fortune to establish an orphanage in Germany, Miss Klingling also willed a large sum "to build and maintain an orphan asylum."[1]

In its heyday, 70 to 80 children lived there. The Warren County Juvenile Court took over the operation of the facility in the 1970s. When we visited, the building was being used as a residential treatment center for young juvenile delinquents.

By the parking lot, a huge tree lay toppled, its roots exposed like those of a half-pulled tooth. Close up, the building looked even more formidable. Under the eaves, I could see holes raggedly stuffed with weeds by the pigeons.

Chris and his associate Kevin, met us at the side door. As we walked down the hall we passed once-elegant woodwork and doors. In Chris's office, I noticed the false drop ceilings, the ill-fitting, scarred doors in the partitions, the linoleum. After explaining how Anne and Rosi and I like to work, all of us went back to the side door and began to wander.

Two steep wooden staircases converged on a central hall. There was a boy sitting on the right stairway, peering down at us in the wedge formed by the ceiling and diagonal slant of the stair. Chris's letter had mentioned that two staff members, during separate incidents, reported seeing a figure in a blue coat in the same spot. A staff member on the second shift saw it duck behind the stairway as if to go down to the basement, and ran after it.

"Why are you out of your bed?" challenged the staff member. But there was no one there. Kevin walking past the exact same spot about 10:00 p.m., saw someone in a blue jacket. The figure raised its right arm over its head and then disappeared.

A plaster medallion at the crossing of the two halls suggested that a chandelier had once hung there. I found that I couldn't walk directly through the space between the staircases. I stood there puzzling over this, trying to picture something to account for it. Had the chandelier come down or the ceiling fallen in?

Chris didn't know of any accidents, but, he said, "there used to be a wall dividing that hall." In the strict regimen of the Orphanage, boys used one staircase, girls used the other. The wall was to keep them apart, to keep them from stealing glances at each other.

Next we all trooped down into the basement. I was uncomfortable there, but figured that was simply because it was dark and cluttered. At one point I felt hemmed in, suffocating, in what I later found out was the detention cell. There were several places that I felt a child's fear and helplessness in the face of adult brutality. In a small closet, I sensed someone begging to be let out. But these seemed to be only memories.

Then Anne and Rosi went into the furnace room. You had to step down several steps to it and walk past the hulking black boiler. I tried, but I couldn't. I took one step over the smooth grey stone threshold, then retreated to the hall.

"I can't go in there," I apologized to the others. "There's something wrong." I was sweating and shivering at the same time, driven back by something dreadful.

In his office, Chris told us of a former resident who lived at the home in its heyday. "She says that a young woman was disciplined, but something went wrong and she died. She says that this young woman was buried in the furnace room. And when they tear down this place, she'll come and show us where.'"

I started up the opposite stairway from the one we came down and found myself face to face with a little girl sitting on the fifth stair down.

"Come up the other way," called Chris. "We keep that door locked." I would too, I thought, if I had to walk through a little girl ghost every time I used the stair.

Going up the stairs to the second floor was like swimming against the tide. Unconsciously we pressed ourselves over to the wall, avoiding the flow of many invisible bodies coming down the stairs. Halfway up the stairs I began to panic in the crush. Behind me Anne said reassuringly, "It's OK."

After slogging our way to the top, the atmosphere was much quieter, much calmer than I would have expected to find in a facility where the young men—no strangers to violence and misery—live and study.

There was nothing in the stark bedrooms but beds you could bounce a quarter on and a few personal possessions in closets without doors. Silhouettes of the human body labeled with the muscle groups hung eerily like corpses in the hall. There was one bedroom I couldn't enter. No special reason; I just couldn't. Later, in our interview with Chris, he told me that staff members and a whole room of residents said they heard screaming in that bedroom. "It sounded like a dog being run over. The boys came running out, terrified." There is another room, he told us, where the boys find their beds creased, with a dent in the pillow, as if someone had laid his head down. Everywhere I got the feeling of children looking out the windows—at what? Their future? Our present?

We trudged up yet another flight of stairs to the third floor. As I looked out a window at the back, I could see some of the outbuildings, including a modern cement block barn. But over it, superimposed, like a transparency, was another barn, an old-fashioned dutch-hipped roof barn, painted white.

"Was there a different barn out back?" I asked. Chris told me that it had been replaced in the 1960s. A young man hung himself in the new barn in 1970.

We continued our third-floor tour. In a green room with stains on the door, a room overlooking the road, a young man stood at the window. He was tall and gangly, obviously a teenager, and he wore pants with suspenders and a collarless white shirt. He looked at me briefly, without interest, then back out the window. He had hung himself—not in the new barn—but when the old barn still stood. He was still here, lonely, waiting for release.

"Is there an attic?" I asked. Kevin nodded and tried to pull open the door. "There is, but it's not real accessible." I could see sticks, bits of dried weed and feathers poking out from under the door.

"I think I can imagine what it's like up there," I said, "Don't bother."

An attic full of birds could be one explanation for things going bump in the night—only it's three floors down to the main floor. Then there's that apparition of the boy in the blue coat...

After our inspection, we went back to Chris's office. I began by saying that most of what haunted the building was memories. So many children, so many joys, so many sorrows—how could the building not have remembered it all?

Chris agrees that nothing feels *directed*. There is no malice, no sense that the spirits are trying to interact with the living. Chris told us other stories about the spirit boy in the blue jacket. A teacher monitoring an after-lunch basketball game, looked up at his second-floor classroom and saw a boy in blue wearing a hat, looking out at him. He thought it was simply one of his regular kids and took off to get the kid out of his room. But all the boys were accounted for outside and staff members had been standing by the stairs the whole time.

Anne said she had been followed all around the orphanage by one spirit. She felt that in addition to the sadness, there had also been a lot of happiness there. The children were trained for a trade, sewing or hairdressing for the girls, farming or woodworking for the boys. For some, this was the only home or kindness they had ever known. Families were sometimes wiped out in epidemics or accidents. This place had provided a stable, if not luxurious, life.

Anne also saw a very strict couple, German, she thought. People who made everything run by the book. Chris nodded. He knew of a particular set of German houseparents who had been rigid disciplinarians.

"For nearly 120 years," Chris said, "this building has been the home for many troubled youths; lost homes, lost families, lost souls. We feel that there are many past memories and experiences of this building from years gone by, that co-exist...with us here today."

A DEADLY BLUE HAZE

Baldwin-Wallace, like most colleges, has its old school spirits. John Baldwin settled in the Berea area in the mid-1800s, intending to found a Methodist commune. The local Methodists didn't think much of the idea, but he did manage to start up the Baldwin Institute, later Baldwin University. In the early 1870s Baldwin University merged with German Wallace College, which occupied the former Methodist Children's Home. That orphanage building was remodeled over the years into what is now Kohler Hall.

Kohler is known as the "freak building," possibly because it is the primary dorm for Conservatory students: musicians, artists, and creative types. The main ghost at Kohler Hall is called "the blue haze." While I suppose we could joke about a "purple haze" being appropriate for the artsy types who live in

Kohler, the fact remains that the mist, which creeps down halls and under doors about two inches off the floor, has been seen by many students and faculty.

A 1990 pamphlet on the Baldwin-Wallace ghosts by the College Historian, Dorothy McKelvey, reports, "One student says he awakened in the middle of the night with a blue haze pressing down on his chest, making it almost impossible for him to breathe." Another resident reported that he was awakened by something sitting on the edge of his bed. Nobody was there, yet the spot where the weight had been was warm.

The "blue haze" ghost always shows up when people are in the hazy state between sleeping and waking: the hypnopompic state, a kind of altered consciousness. Ghostly experiences in Kohler also only occur in the older, original wing of the building.

One serious-minded young woman, a devout Roman Catholic, was in bed one night, reading. She was tired, but didn't feel like getting up to turn off the light. Suddenly, all her blankets slid back towards the foot of the bed, as if about to fall off the end. Sleepily, she just pulled the blankets back up—but she couldn't; it felt as if something was holding the blanket. Suddenly awake, she yanked on the blankets and they slid back up towards her. A second later, they were vigorously pulled off the end of the bed. She grabbed them and pulled, but, held in the grip of *something*, they didn't budge. She jumped out of bed and fled the room.

Brad was sleeping on the floor one night when he felt someone lightly stepping on him. He thought maybe it was his girlfriend's foot or hand. Groggily he rolled over, then felt it again. "What, Tasha?" he asked, waking up. He sat up and realized, Tasha wasn't staying with him that night! He turned on the light and no one was there. "It kind of felt like a cat, like small paws walking over me...." he recalled later.

Michael woke up one night from a nightmare. "Suddenly, I became very much awake—because I sensed that someone else was there in the room with me. I felt like I was being watched—I don't know why...I was scared and prepared to either jump up at the intruder or scream. As I was getting up the nerve to do this, I felt a pull. Someone was pulling my blanket! I was wrapped in it and I was being dragged, with the blanket, to the edge of the bed. I was half-way off the bed, my right hand on the floor, when I squirmed around to face my assailant. There was nothing there."

The Residence Assistant who lived in the next room to Michael was named Toby. One night in 1992, he fell asleep on his couch. He woke up in the middle of the night and saw something in the dim light that shone through his big double windows. It was the black figure of a human creeping across his room. When he looked at it, it froze. For what seemed like hours, they looked at each other. Then the thing "glided" across the room to him. Toby felt a heavy weight on his chest, like it was holding him down. "I couldn't move. I could barely *breathe*. I wanted to scream but I couldn't."

After an eternity, the thing released him and glided through the wall between his room and Michael's. Toby was so terrified he left the building at 3 a.m. and drove to his girlfriend's where he stayed the rest of the night.

A phantom who plays tug-of-war with the blankets; a smothering blue haze—Kohler may not be the "freak" building, but something freakish is certainly going on there.

LIBERTY AND DEATH

The Dayton VA Medical Center was founded in 1867 to take care of disabled Union veterans returning from the Civil War. It was once a showplace, famous for its beautiful gardens, its Sunday afternoon band concerts, its lakes where young men took their young ladies out in rowboats or popped the question in the Tudor gatehouse overlooking the grotto. Now much of the Center is a quiet, rather sad place, a shadow of its former self.

Anne commented on the sadness hanging over the grounds. "It used to be so beautiful. Many of the people sent here were damaged individuals; their lingering spirits are unwholesome. I get the feeling we're being watched."

Anne and I drove the winding roads to Freedom House, a tall, square house painted a dusty rose-beige with dull celadon trim, topped with an oriental-looking cupola. There we were met by Melissa Smith, Program Specialist for the Center and historian for the facility, who hosted our tour. Melissa is a former president of the Civil War Round Table and she is no cloistered historian lost in some romantic historic reverie, but a enthusiastic and practical researcher. Her brisk, sensible attitude towards the Center hauntings was refreshing. Her office was the one room in the building totally clear of ghosts. We joked that she was too sensible to have anything in her office.

Both Freedom House and the building next to it, Liberty House were Designer Showhouses in 1989 and still boast designer touches like handpainted floors, woodwork, and fancy wallpaper. Both seem to have a good deal of ghostly activity.

In one of the Freedom House parlors, Anne and I saw a party going on; the women were dressed in the slanted crinolines of the 1870s; a man in civilian clothes leaned casually with his arm on the marble mantlepiece.

Melissa told us how she and her co-worker Karen were eating their lunch in the Freedom House kitchen when they both heard music on the other side of the building.

"The main room on the other side is not soundproofed and you can hear anything from there. 'Someone's over there,' I said to Karen, 'Can you hear that?'"

Karen could and Melissa went over to check. All the lights were out; all was quiet. She came back to the kitchen and a short time later, they heard the music again. It sounded like modern instrumental background music. There was no one working around the building; nobody outside the building.

The third floor of Freedom House seems the most active. In a back room filled with heating ducts I sensed someone crying. Marcia, who worked at Freedom House for over five years, recalled some of the manifestations there: a light was seen coming down the third floor stairs, footsteps were heard on upper floors when no one was there, that elusive "presence."

"We kept it all to ourselves—until a new staff member moved up on third floor and reported feeling a presence. It got to the place where no one would stay late, after dark, alone in the building. There are still times when the first person to arrive there in the morning has reported that lights that were *off* the night before were *on* when they arrived...the building was locked and the alarm system on." Karen was sitting at her desk on the second floor of Freedom House talking to a colleague standing in the doorway to the hall. Karen watched as a grey mist drifted downstairs from the third floor and down the hall. Her mouth dropped open. Startled, her co-worker turned to see the same grey mist flowing down the hall.

After Freedom House, we visited Liberty House, then being used as a museum. It was filled with dusty glass cases of artifacts, battle flags, and documents. We moved through the building with a kind of hushed wariness. I got a feeling that the presence in the building was trying to keep very still. Perhaps if we could move quickly enough, we'd find it just around the corner. In one upstairs bedroom, we found a mess of plaster fallen from a water-damaged ceiling onto the once-elegant veneered floor.

Just off that room was a tiny room with a window, no bigger than a walk-in closet. As I gazed out the window, I fell into a reverie. "Epilepsy," I found myself thinking. "He had epilepsy, and he shut himself up here when he felt a seizure coming on."

"He" was a middle-aged man in a Civil War uniform. At that time, epilepsy was seen as a kind of insanity. It was the sort of shameful secret a 19th century family would have killed to conceal. Afterwards, as we were discussing this, Anne showed me her notepad on which she had written, "falling sickness"—an old-fashioned term for any kind of seizure.

On a subsequent visit my daughter felt the strong presence of a middle-aged man in the little room. She saw him as being from the 1860s because she sensed he had been in the Civil War. In fact, he lived at the Center in the 1880s, as its Governor. He may have been General Marsena Patrick.

Melissa told us about Brigadier General Patrick. Just before the 1864 Battle of Petersburg, Gen. Patrick felt unwell and sat down under a tree, falling "asleep" immediately. It's possible he had a heart attack because he reported waking with pain in his left shoulder and arm which moved downward. Doctors tortured him with electrical shocks, mercury pills and blistering treatments. The cure was worse than the disease. By September his entire left side was partially paralyzed. After many months of crisis, General Patrick left the service and was granted a disability pension. Perhaps the disease made him subject to seizure-like episodes. I know I felt despair and depression from the man looking out of that tiny window.

Liberty House is now a residence but strange events have continued throughout the renovation. Melissa told me about attempting to videotape oral histories from female veterans. "We had the camera set up on a tripod in Liberty House, but we could not get the equipment to work inside the museum. All we could get was sound, and there was a lot of static so you could barely hear over it. When I saw there was no picture, I took the camcorder back to the media office and told them about the problems we'd had. The guy there tested it out and it worked fine. The same thing happened twice. You could take it *outside* the building and tape anything, but inside, no. We finally had to bring in a tape recorder and just audiotape the interviews."

A narrow servant's staircase runs from the kitchen to the upper floors. As Anne and I picked our way down the stairs, someone came rushing up the stairs at us, shoving rudely by. We looked at each other in astonishment. "Pushy, pushy..." Anne commented.

Our last stop on the tour was the Patient Library. Very little seems to have changed in the Library since it was built. Walking through its rows of old-fashioned bookcases, topped with eerie white plaster busts of Washington, Lincoln and other notables, was like walking back in time. The two tiers of balconies, gleaming with polished wood and brass fittings, were lit by a skylight, which somehow admits a 19th-century light.

"I've been uncomfortable at night at the Patient Library," Melissa admitted. "I spent a lot of time there sorting through the records and artifacts, all the while feeling like somebody was looking over my shoulder."

She finally lost patience with some of the strange noises. "OK," she said, with admirable presence of mind. "Here's the deal. Whoever you are—I'm the historian. If you've got a story, tell me. If not, shut up!"

There is a definite presence in the library. "I got the feeling that someone was standing in the office doorway wondering why I was still working," a library-science intern named Maria once commented to Melissa, "I don't walk back into the building after I have turned out the lights, especially in the winter months."

Seated at an old-fashioned typewriter on a desk in the corner, a woman in a bun, pince-nez, and white blouse looked up at us inquiringly. Melissa has heard other people speak about the ghostly woman who has also been seen standing at the upper windows in the library. I felt a tremor as I looked at the window. Supposedly a small smudged handprint will be found on the window after it has been wiped clean.

Hanging by the typist's desk was a portrait of William Lowell Putnam, a handsome young man, the apple of his mother's eye, a member of the so-called Harvard Regiment. Putnam was killed in his first engagement as a newly commissioned lieutenant in the Union army at Ball's Bluff, Virginia, early in the War. His heartbroken mother established the Putnam Collection at the Patient Library in his memory. Some of the original leather-bound books are still there, stamped with his initials.

"I believe powerful, emotional experiences can leave an echo behind," Melissa said thoughtfully. A mother's lingering grief. A career soldier invalided out of the service, staring sadly, uselessly out the window. A perpetually businesslike librarian. Anne was right; we *were* being watched.

12
GHOSTS OF THE LIVING:
Döppelgangers and *Vardogers*

I'm inclined to think we are all
ghosts—every one of us.
-Henrik Ibsen-

My husband has a good bit of Swedish blood. Almost without exception, when he is away, *something* arrives about a half hour before he does. I'll hear the garage door go up and his motorcycle pull in or the front door open and his golf clubs clank to the floor. It's a bit startling, but comforting, nonetheless, because I know that my living husband will arrive shortly afterwards. In Norway, this is called the *vardoger* — an apparition of a living person who arrives *before* the real person. A *döppelganger* (a German term) is a "double" of a living person, sometimes thought to be an omen of death.

DOUBLE VISION

The following story was sent to me by the late Ken Magnuson. His wife Sue graciously gave me permission to use it, saying he would have liked nothing better than to see his experience in print. The words are as he sent them.

Psychic ability seems to run in my family. For as long as I can remember, my grandmother and my mother have been able to sense danger and deaths of people close to them even when they were separated by great distances. I'll never forget one summer day in 1960 when I was a child. My grandparents were vacationing in Sweden at that time. The phone rang and a look of alarm crossed my mother's face. "Bob," she said to my dad, "your father has died in Sweden." Imagine our surprise when my grandmother told Dad that same news over the phone!

With a family history like mine, and with the experiences I have already described, I should be used to a little bit of strange phenomena, right? Well, nothing in my family background or personal experience prepared me for what I saw one June day in 1982.

That summer I was in graduate school [at Wittenberg] finishing my master's degree. It was a hot summer day and the dorm wasn't air conditioned. For a week I had little piles of index cards spread out on the floor of my room arranged according to the topics I had outlined to prepare my master's thesis. Gradually the piles began to disappear as I assembled the paper. On one particular afternoon I was concentrating very hard on trying to demonstrate the results of my research in the middle of my paper. Occasionally, I glanced down out of my window, watching people enter and leave the dorm, hoping for some inspiration in the wording of my sentences. After several attempts at phrasing, I was becoming increasingly frustrated. I was considering throwing my paper against the opposite wall. Obviously, it was time for a break.

Putting on my running shoes, I decided I'd go out and run a mile to clear my head. Maybe the inspiration would come then. I started out in a jog but gradually built up speed. It felt good to run. There was a nice breeze, and I was beginning to forget all about that frustrating paper.

When I returned to the dorm I definitely felt refreshed. Maybe now I could tackle the paper again. Using my key, I unlocked the dorm room and was halfway to my desk when suddenly I stopped short. There at my desk was my exact double, apparently working on my paper! He appeared to be concentrating very hard. He was almost solid in appearance, and when he turned around, I saw my own face! Something inside me told me that it was not really the true me I was looking at. I felt my identity remained in my own body. After a while the image began to fade. Maybe in five minutes it was totally gone. What in the world was this ghost of myself that I saw?

Since then I have done some reading about this topic. I am of Scandinavian background. Seeing one's own double is accepted in Norwegian and Swedish folklore. Perhaps, as one book I read indicated, I had been concentrating so hard that I left behind a little field of energy which I was able to see as an image. Whatever the cause, I believe the most unusual ghost I have ever seen was my own ghost.

DOUBLE TROUBLE

In 1977, Donna was a junior at Ohio State University, living at home in Columbus with her widowed mother. She slept in a makeshift bedroom in the basement, her bed directly beneath the front porch and front door.

"The routine was for my mother to go out several nights a week to visit her boyfriend, come tearing back in around 11:00 p.m., come tromping (for a small lady she could really tromp) up the side walk, enter the house and slam the door shut. The door had to be slammed, otherwise it wouldn't close properly.

"One night I had just turned out the light and settled down to sleep when I heard footsteps come stomping up the front sidewalk. My only thought was that Mom had made an early night of it, as it was only about 9:00 p.m."

Steps sounded on the porch. Donna heard the door open, although she later recalled that she hadn't heard the usual jangle of door keys, then she heard the door being firmly slammed shut. Donna went to sleep.

She slept until about 6:30 a.m. the next morning, then went upstairs to put the kettle on for tea. A few minutes later, her mother's Chevy Caprice came roaring into the driveway.

"Mom jumped out of her car and came running up the steps. When she got into the house she looked at me sheepishly and started apologizing for not getting home until morning."

At first Donna laughed to herself—here was her 45-year-old widowed mother justifying her behavior to her college-age daughter. Then Donna stopped dead in mid-sip.

"I remembered thinking she had been home all the time. To this day I cannot explain why I heard all the activities of the night before. My mom said I was lucidly dreaming, but I had just turned out the light and was very much awake when I heard someone coming up the walk and enter the house."

The people of the north have a name for this arrival phenomenon—where a person is seen or heard arriving shortly before they actually do. In Norway it is called the *Vardoger*, which means "forerunner."

Or perhaps Donna heard her mother's anxious astral projection coming home.

THE GREAT PRETENDER

Something in our house on Pearl Street in Marion would take the form of my older sister Stacey, mock her, and *be* her [wrote Kaalem]. And it was damn good at it! The first time was late at night about 12:30 or 1 a.m. Dad was at work and my Mom was the only one awake. Mom was lying in her room with her door open, talking to my aunt on the phone. Mom saw my sister, wearing a favorite nightgown, walk by the door, headed for the bathroom. Mom thought nothing of it, until Stacey never walked back by the door. The longer she and my aunt talked, the more concerned Mom got. Had Stacey fallen or gotten sick in the bathroom? She told my aunt to hang on; she had to check on Stacey. In the bathroom, the sink was bone dry, and the toilet wasn't running. Everything looked untouched. "Well," she thought, "maybe she got back by the door without me noticing."

When Mom got to Stacey's doorway, she found her sound asleep, lying on top of the covers, as usual, but wearing a *different* nightgown.

The second time, I was in my bedroom, in the middle of the day. I wasn't comfortable in the room at night and usually never slept there. My room had been a sunporch at the back of the house and you actually had to pass through the bathroom to get to my room. I knew Stacey was in her room at the front of the house, so I relaxed. I was playing a record on my portable record player.

Then I saw Stacey leaving the bathroom, headed back to her room. She wore a red robe and a towel on her head. I could see her wet hair slicked back under the towel. Five or ten minutes later I went to borrow a record from Stacey. I went through the bathroom, down the open hallway and stepped into her room. The room was very cold, very empty, and there was no towel, no robe, lying anywhere. My heart began to pound because I knew she hadn't had time to get away. I gave myself one last chance: I thought surely she was downstairs. I ran into the kitchen where Mom was.

'What's wrong?' she asked.

'I'm looking for Stac!'

'She's at work.'

'No, she's not! Did she just leave?'

'No, she was at work before you got up this morning.'

So what it was that I saw in my sister's red robe, I don't know!

THE GHOST OF CHILDHOOD PAST

Jeanine may have met her own ghost in a time of crisis.

She explained, "My first real apartment was in a converted motel on Rt. 127 going towards Hamilton just outside of Seven Mile. I had lived there a couple of months when I was talking to my friend Rhonda about some problems with a boyfriend. The apartment had been made out of two single motel rooms. There was no real door between the bedroom and the living room, just a wall that only went half-way up. As Rhonda was on her way out the door, still talking to me, this girl just walked from behind this half wall and looked at me. She wore a brand of clothes called "Garanimals" popular in the 1980s: lavender shorts, a sleeveless top with tiny stripes of navy-blue, yellow, and purple. She had shoulder-length dirty-blond hair, pulled over to one side with a plastic barrette. She was tanned, but kind of grungy looking, like she had been playing around in the dirt. Her mannerisms were like an 8- or 9-year-old, but she was lanky, bony, and tall—about the height of a 12-year-old. She seemed really nervous and scared. She fidgeted a lot. She looked right at me.

"I just stared at her. Rhonda realized I was no longer paying attention to her and she got upset. I could hear everything Rhonda was saying to me, but I didn't know how to get her to notice the thing standing beside her. When I talked to Rhonda a couple of weeks later, I asked if I had said anything to anyone in the room. She said I hadn't, but I felt like I was communicating with the girl. Mentally I asked her,

'Do you want to go with Rhonda?'

She shook her head vigorously, 'No!' Like 'No way I'm going to go with this woman.'

'Well, you can stay here, then,' I thought. Then the girl just disappeared. She was there and then not there.

"After that I could hear the girl knocking around in the cabinets, looking in the fridge. She knocked a lot on the wood panels of the stereo console. She didn't bother me too much. I did have to inform her she had to be quiet while I was asleep during the day. I don't know where she came from; or why she was there."

As I got Jeanine's story, I had a sudden hunch: did the young girl look like Jeanine when *she* was that age?

"I've thought about that," Jeanine said. "It did look kind of like me when I was that age. I was always real nervous, shy and fidgety. I spent a lot of time alone as a kid and didn't really like social situations. I was tall, had that dirty-blonde hair, although I parted mine in the middle. But if it was me, *why* was it me?"

It's said that when we get into stressful situations, we sometimes revert to childish ways of behaving. I wonder if the stressful time Jeanine was having with her boyfriend might have created a ghost of her own childhood, a literal shadow of her former self.

13

MURDER MOST PHANTOM:
Ghostly murder victims

Other sins only speak; murder shrieks out.
-John Webster-

One of the most common stories in ghostly folklore is the murder victim who cannot rest until his body is properly buried or her murderer is brought to justice. Blood cries out from the ground for vengeance.

DEATH IN THE POT

Although Nanette Young and her friends had grown up with the story of Lucy Cobb, the crazy mushroom lady, they always thought it was just a local legend—until one fall afternoon.

While trotting on horseback towards the ruins of Lucy's Inn on what was once a stagecoach road, Nanette and Jackie's horses were spooked by the sounds of dogs fighting. As they approached a crumbling wall, they saw two big dogs wrestling over a large bone. A hiker emerged from the dense woods, whistling and calling for his dogs. He took the bone. The two curious women dismounted to see what was going on and to talk to the hiker.

Their first impression was that the bone belonged to a deer. Looking at it closer, they realized that it was a human bone. As the three talked about the area and its many ghost stories, they also realized that they were on the site of what had once been Lucy Cobb's Inn.

In the mid-1800s, Lucy Cobb and her family operated a small hostelry along the Sandy and Beaver Canals in southeast Columbiana County. Lucy was a large-boned, homely Dutch woman. She had few friends and rarely saw anyone except the travelers and canal workers she fed with her excellent pies and stews.

She was smitten by a young stone cutter, Tommy Ware, and tried to show him how she felt by secretly leaving special sweets on his window sill. One day, as she brought him a cherry tart, she saw Tommy and Sarah, a lovely young woman from the village, kissing as sweethearts do. Furious, Lucy rushed home swearing revenge on the man whom she felt had betrayed her.

That night Lucy dug two graves beside a stone wall in her garden where poisonous mushrooms grew. Covering her hand with her apron, for they were so deadly the poison could be absorbed through the skin, she picked a pocketful of Death-Angel mushrooms.

The next day when Lucy brought by her usual treats, Tommy introduced Sarah as his fiancee. Smiling, Lucy wished them a long and happy life and invited them to dinner to celebrate their betrothal. She served them one of her special stews, subtly flavored with wild mushrooms. The after-dinner conversation was cut short, however, as Sarah's cup fell from her paralyzed fingers and she rolled to the floor. Startled, Tommy bent over her, and also collapsed, a black foam on his lips. Lucy dragged the two convulsed bodies to their garden graves and covered them over with moss and leaves so cleverly no one would have ever known they were there.

It was believed in the village that Tommy and Sarah had eloped. If anyone suspected Lucy, who grew more and more reclusive as time passed, they didn't mention it. But the people of the village didn't accept any dinner invitations either.

Jackie and Nanette wondered if the old bone came from one of Lucy's victims. They went back the next day to re-examine the soil. Oddly, there was no evidence that they had just been there. Where there should have been hoofprints, footprints, and fresh-dug dirt, only mushrooms dotted the shadowed hillside. Had Lucy's land once more covered all trace of human passage?

Some months later, Nanette and Jackie met the same hiker and his dogs. He had taken the bone to the coroner who felt it was indeed the legbone of a male, age eighteen to twenty, dating from the 1830s or 40s. Somewhere under the deadly mushrooms, two young lovers'graves await the discovery of the truth.

THE GUENTHER HOUSE GHOST

On the western edge of the village of Macedon stood the Guenther House. Operated by John Guenther and his sons, brawls and poisonous home-brew were the regular bill of fare. One New Year's Eve, a dance was just getting lively when a liquored-up stock drover boasted in his cups of having $500 about his person.

A young man named John Young was sober enough to notice that Guenther was plying the drover with even more liquor. After the party broke up, Young hung about outside in the darkness. As he watched a lighted upstairs window, he heard a sickening thud, like an ax makes when it smashes into the skull of a butchered hog. Then the light was put out.

Later, he saw three men stagger out of the inn carrying something suspiciously man-sized. They returned quickly, empty-handed. Young melted away into the darkness. The next day he heard the news: the drover had disappeared, leaving behind his saddlebags, which did *not* contain any $500, and the tavern's well had been filled in. The local people could put two and two together as well as the next person, but they feared the quick-tempered Guenther and his strapping sons, so they said nothing.

Young enlisted in the Union Army shortly after this incident. When he returned from the war, the Guenthers, who had been notoriously sympathetic to the South, had fled to Canada.

Learning that they were gone, Young told his story to some friends and the group started excavating the well. When they reached a depth of 16 feet, Young suffered a heart attack, which so unnerved his friends that they gave up.

Guenther House was soon abandoned and was shunned by the locals. No tenant stayed for more than a few months. It was said that lights could be seen moving about upstairs. If you hung about long enough, you might hear the thud of a ghostly ax on a man's skull and the ghostly splash of a body down a well.[1]

DEATH IN EDEN

It was 1927—the age of jazz, flappers, and bathtub gin. On the morning of October 6, George Remus, Cincinnati's bootleg king was fresh out of jail after serving a two-year term for bootlegging. While he was languishing in jail, his wife Imogene had taken up with one of the prohibition agents who put George behind bars. George naturally felt hurt and betrayed, especially since he had given his wife a hoard of diamond jewelry for safekeeping while he was "away."

Imogene had a date with George—in divorce court—that October morning. Instead, he pursued her by taxi to Eden Park, chased her into the gazebo by Mirror Lake, and instead of complimenting her on her new Paris-model hat or asking for a reconciliation, shot her dead.

Crazy like a fox, George threw his gun into the woods where it was missed by the police, but found years later by a child on an Easter egg hunt. George was found "not guilty by reason of insanity," sent to Lima State Hospital for a 6-month "cure," and then released.

The injustice was enough to make a ghoul cry—and haunt. Imogene's petulant ghost, fashionably dressed in black silk and that smart Parisian hat, still lingers in the gazebo overlooking Mirror Lake. If you see her there, ask her what she did with the diamonds.[2]

THE STONEY CREEK SPECTRE

That day in 1825, Daniel*, the caretaker of Stoney Creek Church had come to trim the grass among the graves. With his scythe and his long beard, he could have been Father Time himself. He scythed his way towards the back of the churchyard, then paused to mop his head with his handkerchief. The shadow of a huge oak reached out to him. It was one of the oldest trees in Adams County. He saw someone lying up against the tree as if asleep. A tramp, he thought. I better run him off, we don't want that riff-raff around here. He walked boldly up to the tree.

There Daniel froze at the sight. It was a man, his clothing stiff with clotted blood and swarming with flies. He's got no head, thought Daniel stupidly. Coming closer, he made a horrifying discovery. The head had not been cut from the man's body with an ax or knife. The twisted, wrinkled skin and the snapped backbone pointed to the unthinkable: that the man's head had been ripped from his living shoulders. Daniel fled.

The local authorities brought out their tracking dogs, but the stranger's head was never found. The lack of blood on the ground by the oak seemed to show that the man had been killed elsewhere. Authorities were left with an unidentifiable, unclaimed body, and the mystery of what kind of creature had the strength to rip a man's head clean off.

Daniel wrapped the man's body in a sheet and buried him in an unmarked grave near the oak tree. It is whispered that if you venture too close to the tree on the wrong night, you'll see something strange under the tree: a headless body bound in a sheet, a wriggling, human-size worm, sobbing wordlessly as the wind moans over a hole in the stump where the head should be.[3]

THE SHRIEKING GHOST OF WHITE LADY POINT**

You won't find White Lady Point on a modern map of the Ohio River. But the riverfolk who've spent their lives on the water could tell you exactly how to find the place. They know where the narrow path leads down through scrub willow to the water's edge. Unless it's broad daylight, though, no one will volunteer to show you the way.

The story of White Lady Point begins not so long ago, in the early part of the 19th century. It was a different river then. Today's Ohio has been tamed, contained by embankments and levees, robbed of its current by a series of dams.

Back then the river ran free and wild. Primeval forest blanketed the hills. There were still bear and wolves, bobcats and panthers hunting by the river's banks. When the sun set, and no moon cast its silver light on the water the river was a black ribbon flowing into the unknown.

According to the log book of the paddle-wheeler, *Kanawha Gal*, a deckhand was the first to hear the screams. The steamboat was tied up for the night on the Kentucky side of the river, two days' journey above Cincinnati. It was late October and the packet carrier was on its way from Louisville to Pittsburgh. The captain was quickly summoned. He, too, heard the frantic shrieks.

The voice seemed to be a woman's, though sound heard at a distance across water sometimes plays tricks. It could have been a child, they said. Both men also heard another voice—coarser, masculine—above the screams.

Then suddenly — silence.

The battered body of Mary Fisk was found by a hunter the next morning. She was dressed in an ankle-length white gown, spattered with blood, floating face down in the shallows where the mouth of a wooded cove enters the Ohio. Her blond hair was tangled and matted with mud.

The Fisk cabin, located atop a nearby hill, was in shambles. Household goods were strewn about. What little

**As told by Jim McGuire in *The Miami Sunday News*.

furniture the place contained was overturned or broken. There was blood everywhere.

It was evident Mary Fisk had put up a terrific fight. But she'd been no match for her attacker. A single bloody hand-print stamped in Mary's blood on the wall gave mute testimony to her attacker's size. No man who compared his hand that day with the one written in blood could match its span. It was the handprint of a giant.

The tragedy of the murder worsened when it was discovered that Mary's six-year-old son was missing. Search parties scoured the woods for days, but no trace of little Daniel Fisk was ever found.

Calhoun Fisk, Mary's husband, was leading a party of land speculators up the Levisa Fork of the Big Sandy. He wasn't due home for another week, so neighbors carried Mary's body up the hill to the small cabin. They cleaned and dressed her in crinoline. A grave was dug and the simple wooden coffin was lowered into the rich earth. A few days later a young guide returned home to learn he'd been widowed and his son mysteriously taken.

The murder of Mary Fisk was never solved. Little Daniel Fisk disappeared forever. Whoever—or whatever—came out of that October night left nothing behind but a lone, gigantic handprint. It might have ended there, another incident of unsolved frontier violence. By rights, only historians should know the tale.

But the story is alive—and maybe something else is, too. After Mary's killing the riverfolk began seeing something along the stretch of shoreline where the body was found. The reports generally record the same thing—a fair-haired woman in white, arms outstretched, mouth open wide as if screaming. She rises from the mist and floats above the water.

Newspapers and regional histories have carried accounts of these sightings for years. For example, two fishermen nearly tore the hull out of their boat, grounding it in a panicked moment of terrified escape. Said one, "We saw her plain as day. She came right towards us and we didn't wait around. We were going full-throttle when we hit the bank!"

The specter came to be known as the white lady, and the river pilots called the place White Lady Point. They pointed it out to passengers during the day—and steered as far away from it as possible during the night.[4]

WORKING-CLASS STIFFS:
More ghosts in the workplace

They rest from their labours.
-Book of Common Prayer-

GRAVEYARD SHIFT

I knew Vern from my church. He was a quiet, analytical sort, a crackerjack volleyball player, and definitely not a guy I expected to even think about ghosts. So his question one night at church was a complete surprise. He scuffed his toe a little nervously.

"Do you ever visit haunted places?"

"Sure do," I said, wrestling with a bag of angel wings for the Christmas pageant. "Whatcha got?"

"Well, I manage this property down in Wilmington and the people there say they've been having problems. Would you come check it out?"

Ghosts were the last thing on my mind with all the Christmas preparations, but I said, "Sure. My only rule is that nobody is to tell me anything about it. Don't give me any details—has anything been seen?"

This is usually the only question I ask people because I find if anything has been seen, I've got a better chance of having a good session at the site. The answer was yes.

It was a sunny, late spring day when Vern and Christy, the property manager, and I finally drove down to the modern warehouse facility. Vern assured me that the employees had been briefed and would not say anything until I was finished.

I shook hands with Ed, a company Vice President, a bearded man in a handknit sweater who looked like he belonged behind the counter of a bookstore/coffeehouse in Seattle. I explained the rules: I would walk around and take notes. They could follow but nobody should interfere or tell me anything until I was done.

Before I began, I went into the restroom. I hadn't expected anything ghostly to happen, but as I sat there, the walls began to cave in around me. It was a dizzying, unsettling sensation, but intriguing. It isn't every day I get buried alive in a toilet stall. As I later found out from Ed and Vern, a worker was buried in a cave-in as the facility was being built and was rescued barely in time.

I stepped through the door into the warehouse area. It was one huge room full of shelving and pallets arranged in lines with aisles running crossways creating a grid pattern. Just to my right was a sort of dead-end hall with some pallets and other trash stacked at the end. I wandered down the hall and was suddenly utterly exhausted. I propped myself against the wall to keep from collapsing and closed my eyes. I had a weird sensation of something poking at me, trying to get through.

I finally pulled myself together, hoisted myself away from the wall, and walked beyond a wire-caged room to an isolated desk I was later told was the receiving department. I sank into the chair and was startled to hear a man's voice exclaim,

"It's not fair! It's not fair!"

I began to get a picture of the speaker. He was a young man, quite modern, dressed in a work uniform—like a grey version of the UPS uniform, including a jacket, and heavy work shoes or boots. His hair was darkish; his eyes were a very bright blue. He had a kind of hard-to-describe good looks—conventionally attractive, but too bland, too lacking in character, for my taste. His face was a little puffy around the chin and jawline, perhaps from too much drinking.

The picture was strangely clear. I even got a job description. He was management, yet he was wearing a uniform instead of a tie. He was blue collar, but not just a worker—he was higher up than that—or liked to think he was.

And he thought he was God's gift to women! Cocky, swaggering, completely sure of himself, the sort of guy who has women running after him—and brags about it, the kind of guy who tells dirty jokes to female employees, the guy with the too-friendly hands. At Aisle 4, I caught a glimpse of him, leaning up against a post, his hips thrust arrogantly forward.

The entire warehouse area was dark. I kept looking up to see if bulbs were out, but it looked to me as if all lights were lit; this was a different sort of darkness. At Gate D, something very strong stood in my path and I had to dodge around it. Along one wall was a row of small glassed-in offices. The first one was OK. In the next one, I felt an intense electric tingling sensation. Later Ed's wife, Cindy, a department manager, told me this was her office.

At the end of the warehouse, I turned left. There was a door, apparently to some offices, which gave me the shudders. I began to walk up the aisle, making a loop back to my starting point. I glanced over to my left. The young man was an aisle over, walking parallel to me, pacing with an exaggeratedly large step as if mocking me. Halfway down the wall aisle, I felt him—he was so angry he wanted to kick the wall, to stomp on the floor. I kept walking, keeping a wary eye on him. He had an air of unpredictable impulse about him, a what-the-hell streak that some women might find attractive. It scared me. I blew out a deep breath of relief as I stepped back through the warehouse door into the reception area.

We all went back into Ed's office. He sat quietly behind his desk, fingers steepled, while I gave him the details: the clothes, the coloring, the attitude, the harrassment. I theorized that the ghost had died suddenly and was resentful that he was still stuck on the job. The longer I talked, the more nervous I got. Ed wasn't saying anything. He wasn't nodding. He looked totally bored and noncommittal. I began to fidget. I must really be off base, I thought. They've probably all seen a

ghostly woman in white instead of this guy. I've made an
absolute idiot of myself...."

"That's all I got," I finished, "I'm sorry I can't be more
helpful. What have you experienced?"

Ed unsteepled his hands, sat up, and smiled.

"Well, that's exactly what we've always felt about the
ghost," he said, and I slumped into my chair, relieved. "You've
described what some employees here believe they've been
seeing and feeling as well as the places he's most active. We've
always felt that he was sort of middle management or supervi-
sor-like. And for some reason the ghost seems busiest on
weekends!"

The current business moved into the building in July of
1995. Right from the start, strange things began to happen.
Something kept dialing 911, which the dispatcher found very
eerie since the building was empty. Finally the police called
Ed and Cindy to come down to the building where the 911 calls
originated.

"As we entered, we could hear the slamming of pallets. I
heard a door slam, then the sound of machinery running. After
a minute or so, the door opened again, and the equipment
sounded like it turned itself back off. But nothing was actually
running. We were the only ones there. The doors that sounded
like they were slamming were locked. Things were very busy
that day!"

For the next two months strange things went on: toilets
flushed when no one was in the bathroom. Employees caught
glimpses of someone out of the corners of their eyes. The
lights, especially in the area of Cindy's office, changed colors.
Normally off-white, they changed randomly from blue to
orange to green, baffling electricians. Unplugged computers
turned on and displayed gibberish on their screens. Music
played from unplugged radios. Finally, motion sensors were
installed in the building.

On one occasion, police were dispatched to the building
when the alarms showed some type of intrusion attempt. The
first one, they dismissed as a bird flying through the motion

detectors. The next time, Ed came down to the building to check. Again, the officers were discounting the alarm and someone made a remark to Ed about "must be the ghost you have in the building."

"As soon as he said that, *all* the alarms went off in the building. I called the security company to tell them it was a false alarm," Ed told me. "They said that their sensors showed motion throughout the building. It appeared to them that all the doors to the building were opening and closing even though we were there and could see that nothing was really happening."

Two days later, on another 911 call, police released a search dog. The dog immediately climbed onto the desk with the telephone to which the police had traced the 911 calls. The dog then ran to the returns area, then to aisle 4, where an employee had been touched. From there, he went back to the vacant offices where Ed and Cindy first heard doors opening. Then the dog parked himself in the bathroom and stared at the ceiling. His handler gave him several commands, but the animal finally had to be physically dragged out.

The apparition seems to target women. Cindy and Nichole were alone in the warehouse one night when they heard a man's voice yelling at them. Other women working the lines have heard a male speaking to them. Joyce heard someone say a name. She shut down her conveyor belt to ask Angi, the woman next to her, "Why are you calling me Margaret?"

"I didn't say anything."

"Yes, you did, I heard you say 'Margaret'!"

They got rather huffy about it. Employees also find themselves quarreling over missing items. Some women have felt a hand pulling on their clothes.

"Your skin will crawl," said Cindy.

Shelly told me that she was working in aisle 4 when something tugged at her shirt and put a hand on her waist! I asked her to show me exactly what had happened and where. She obligingly walked down the aisle towards the spot. I followed her briskly, then began to walk slower and slower. I stopped dead about nine feet from her and she bent over, posed, as she had been when she felt the hand. The ghost was standing behind her, leering, pretending to pinch her bottom.

The others laughed as they saw me stop, but I shook my head, "He's right behind you, Shelly. I'll stay where I am."

I thought, "This guy must have kept the Human Resources Department busy with sexual harrassment complaints!"

In another terrifying incident, the entire end of a row of steel pallet racks appeared to lift off the floor two feet without disturbing the stock on the shelves. In this same area, employees have heard a shrill whistle pass right by their ears, and turned to catch a glimpse of the ghost some ten feet away.

The workers I talked to seemed intrigued by the whole thing and were eager to share their stories with somebody who wouldn't think they were crazy. Ed says there are still some non-believers, but most people take the ghost seriously, "Some even say, 'Geez, he's just somebody we're going to have to work with,' and they find humor in it. He's just working another shift."

So who was this guy? I didn't find out that particular day, but as I was finishing this story, I called Ed for a few more details. He referred me to Freeda, the receptionist who had told her husband about my visit and had described the ghost to him.

"That's Bernie*!" Freeda's husband exclaimed. He told of a young man who worked in maintenance for a business just around the corner from Ed's building. "He was a cocky little...," he said. "He always thought he deserved more pay and a better job title than he had." Freeda knew Bernie's mother and told me, "He drank a lot and had quite an attitude. He was spoiled rotten. Whatever Bernie wanted, Bernie got."

But in the end, Bernie didn't get what he wanted. His wife was seeing another man and Bernie, perhaps in a fit of drunken spite, hung himself in their home.

"It's not fair!" the ghost had cried. At the time I had jokingly wondered if he resented working weekends. Suddenly it became apparent just why the ghost with the attitude problem had a reason to be resentful.

THE GHOST IN THE LIBRARY TOWER

In the 1890s steel magnate Andrew Carnegie began giving away his fortune to build public libraries. He first endowed places that had influenced his early life: in Ohio that meant Sandusky, East Liverpool—and Steubenville, where the 15-year-old Carnegie had been a telegrapher.

The Steubenville Library was designed to be a $50,000 building with a commanding peaked roof, massive twin chimneys and a 105-foot stone clock tower. Construction began in 1901 in Steubenville's South End; the mammoth building loomed over the modest homes surrounding it. Halfway through the project, money ran out and Carnegie was asked for a supplemental grant of $12,500; he generously gave it. When the building was nearly finished, it became apparent that the money wouldn't stretch to buy the four-sided clock for the tower. A third appeal to Carnegie was met with silence. A Library Board member later reported that Carnegie had remarked, "Let them buy watches!"

The enormous building opened on March 12, 1902. The first librarian of the new Carnegie Library was Ellen Summers Wilson of Albany, New York. When she first took up her new post, her office stood behind the main library desk. However, when the trustees complained of having to climb the 31 steps up the spiral staircase to the Trustee Room in the clock tower, Miss Wilson's office was moved to the former Trustee Room. Two years later, she died of a heart attack, possibly brought on by the 62 steps required to get from her office to the circulation desk.

Immediately stories began to circulate about strange noises in the attic of the library, of creaking sounds and footsteps heard from the unoccupied attic. The ghost of Miss Wilson, of course, keeping an eye on things from her lofty domain.

Today the Ghost in the Library Attic is practically an institution in Steubenville; a staff sign on the attic door proclaims, "Home of the Library Ghost." Strangely creaking beams and odd breathing noises from the cooling ducts still haunt the library. Today the attic houses modern air condition-

ing equipment that mysteriously turned itself off for no
apparent reason—until the controls were moved downstairs. Is
it the ghost of Miss Wilson, annoyed at her banishment to the
Tower? Or Andrew Carnegie, trying to pinch some pennies?

ANNIE

There is a group home in Jackson County where one of the
residents has lived there *much longer* than any of the others!
She is called Annie. The big, three-story house started life as a
middle-class 19th century home. In 1977, it was taken over by
the Volunteers of America for use as a group home for institu-
tionalized women. It has an old-fashioned porch, "big enough
to have a good time on," said former worker Anne. There are
also pocket doors, gorgeous woodwork and moulding, and
stained glass on the landing with twin portraits said to be of the
builder's daughter. A servant's staircase runs from the side
door and kitchen up to the attic, which, says Anne, "was not a
comfortable place to be. The energy there was more than I was
willing to deal with."

Many people have heard footsteps where no one is
walking. One resident often talks like she's having a conversation with somebody. If you ask her, "Who are you talking to?",
she'll reply, "Oh, him there," waving a hand.

"Who?"

"Oh well, they're gone now," she'll say vaguely and
wander off.

Some of the workers hear their names called.

Marlene told me, "All the ladies were at camp during the
week and nobody else was in the house. But I distinctly heard
someone calling my name. I thought maybe someone had their
arms full and wanted me to open the door, but nobody was at
the back door and nobody was at the front door.

"I started to think, 'Who else is here?' But the voice only
called once. It was a woman's voice and I didn't recognize it.

"Once when I was working in the office after everyone else
was in bed, I felt a presence behind me. You know how you

know when somebody has snuck up behind you? I thought it was one of the residents wanting something, so I turned around and no one was there—visibly. But for the next 10 minutes I could feel someone looking over my shoulder. There was no definite noise, just a friendly presence. I figured it was Annie. I was surprised; I'd never felt like this before. But I tried not to be afraid. I never thought any harm would come of it.

"One morning, all the residents had gone off on the bus to their sheltered workshop where they work during the day. Kendra and I were in the kitchen, cleaning up, when we heard a loud knocking coming from the floor, right near my feet. I could feel the vibrations jarring my feet at each rap like someone knocking on the ceiling of the basement with a broomstick. I asked Kendra who else was home. Nobody was. Starting in the basement, we checked at all the doors and windows in the whole house."

"Once Kendra was there alone, making a cake. Hours later, when she was in another room, she heard a buzzing noise from the kitchen. She went into the kitchen and found the mixer switched on, bouncing around on the counter. She watched till it fell on the floor, unplugging itself."

Only a few people have actually *seen* Annie, who apparently likes to keep a low profile. Lora and Kim saw her wearing a long blue jumper. She had short, dark, greying hair. Kim was trying to sleep in the back servant's bedroom in the attic when Annie yanked the covers off her bed.

Anne moved in as a house parent in 1977, when the house was first turned into a group home.

"I never felt alone in this house, *never*. There has always been energy at the group home. I knew it the first moment I walked into the house. The group home was a big, old house and houses talk. There was a cold spot in the stairwell of the attic. I always had to walk through it and it wasn't explainable by drafty windows.

"I consistently smelled chocolate chip cookies baking. It always happened when I was by myself so I couldn't ask others about it. I never saw anybody. I think I was too afraid to really open up. But about two years later, I bought a house two doors up from the house and I think Annie has checked on me here from time to time.

"One night I was lying awake, facing and talking to my husband in bed, when something touched my back. I could feel the outstretched palm and the fingertips as they brushed me. It got my attention!

"One evening I was downstairs and I could hear somebody walking on the furnace grate. I thought my children were out of bed. I went up to see and when I walked into the hallway, I walked right through her cold spot—or she walked through me—and every hair on my body bristled. Someone was there. I just figured it was Annie."

At one point Kim tried to research the history of the house, but failed at every attempt. She checked plat maps and old records and tried to interview a relative of the former owner. This person clammed up and would not answer questions. Maybe Annie—if she is the ghost—doesn't want the living to know her story. Even a ghost is entitled to a little privacy.

THE BREWER'S GHOST

In life, Jake Halm, the town of Bryan's first and only brewmaster, was a kindly man, concerned with little except perfecting his craft. In death, he remains a most inoffensive ghost, wanting only to be left alone in the dark with his spectral kegs under Beer Cellar Hill.

In pre-Prohibition days, when beer was seen as a solid, refreshing beverage, Halm was famed throughout the county for the quality of his beer. The Anti-Saloon League, however, viewed him as they would the Antichrist.

Halm brought his brewing secrets from Germany where his family had brewed Pilsener for generations. He also had some theories of his own about aging his products and dug a vast cellar under a hill one mile west of Bryan's Court Square on what is now US 6. He spent his life there, testing the contents of kegs and casks and tuns, ever alert for leaks.

He would say, "In anoder year dot vill be gute, in two years it vill be besser, in dree years I let mine customers haf it . . . *einz, zwei, drei.*"

While his fans were legion, the anti-alcohol forces were gathering strength and numbers. Preachers denounced Halm's hellbrews from the pulpit. God was called upon to strike the hill with earthquakes, lightning, and mudslides and to afflict Halm himself with leprosy, boils, and bad breath. The local children were warned away from the hill where they sledded in winter and gathered wild strawberries in summer, and filled with dark warnings about the demons who were the brewmaster's assistants.

Tragically, Halm was killed in a terrible accident at the Fountain City Brewery in 1883 after becoming entangled in some machinery. His body was horribly mangled as it was caught between two cog-wheels; his left arm torn off at the shoulder.

Prayers of thanksgiving were offered in some churches because the brewery had shut down. Halm's trade secrets had died with him, and Beer Cellar Hill was emptied out.

The cavern beneath the hill became a magnet for local boys who went in to chase the rats, fattened to the size of cats by the leftover grain and malt. The remaining empty barrels sprouted mushrooms in the dank cellar and water trickled through the widening cracks of the masonry.

Prohibition was enacted in 1920, to protect the God-fearing American public from the evils of drink and it was proclaimed that John Barleycorn was dead. But John Barleycorn was only dormant. He soon arose again, and so, apparently, did Jake Halm. About the same time that the brewmaster's former customers began to rot their livers with bootleg liquor, his ghost showed itself in the cellar. Several boys saw it, and heard the slow pad of feet, the hollow rolling of kegs, and a heavy German voice repeating, "In anoder year it vill be gute... *einz, zwei, drei.*"

Ever since the repeal of Prohibition, it is said that Halm walks in the hollow hill. On still nights you might hear the soft bubbling of the mash. If your nose is keen, you might get a wiff of malt. And if your ears are tuned to yet another level, you may even hear Halm's ghost counting out the years.[1]

SURVIVALS AT THE MAJESTIC

A wrought-iron arch, festive with lights, crosses the narrow street in front of the Majestic Theatre in Chillicothe. The arch, bearing an uncanny resemblance to those that mark the entrances of old-time graveyards, is the sole survivor of a set of five that spanned High St. in Columbus in the early 1900s.

There are many such survivals at the Majestic as I found on my tour. Marti Oyer, Office Assistant, started me off with a history of the Theatre. It stands on the site of the first bank erected in Chillicothe. When a fire destroyed the bank, the Masons bought the land and built The Masonic Opera House in 1853. The theatre seats were built on wheeled platforms that could be pushed back so patrons could dance or roller skate. Many celebrities played the Masonic Opera House, later the Majestic: Milton Berle, Sophie Tucker, Laurel and Hardy.

Today the crimson velvet curtain is embroidered with a curliqued M for Mason or Majestic. Carved and gilded fans, a wreath and musical instruments shine around the stage. As I wandered around the theatre, I kept turning around to see who it was that was staring at us from the tiny landing by the projection booth, known as the Crow's Nest.

In the balcony the maroon-and-yellow palmetto-frond carpet is still bright. The seats are duplicates of the originals. One section is filled with the original surviving "lovers' seats"—double chairs for cuddling couples.

Beneath the stage are the dressing rooms, their ceilings no higher than a crypt. The whitewashed brick walls were strangely familiar. Then it hit me: grave vaults in New Orleans.

Up on stage, Managing Director Gilda Lynch, took over with a grisly tale of the days when the Majestic witnessed a real-life tragedy. At nearby Camp Sherman, hundreds of young soldiers gasped their lives away as the Spanish Influenza epidemic swept through their ranks in 1918. So many died so quickly. Health officials needed a temporary morgue. The dead were taken in wagons to the Majestic where their bodies were stacked in the dressing rooms and hallways like cordwood until the embalmers could get to them. The embalmers worked under the stage lights and pumped the corpses' blood into a neighboring alley, still known as "Blood Alley." Gilda's great-great-uncle staged a come-back. Even though he was toe-tagged for dead; he regained consciousness before being taken to the theater. A startled nurse revived him. He survived.

It may be one of these soldiers' corpses that appeared on stage during a local theatre group's production several years ago. They were filming the play and through the viewfinder, the cameraman was mystified to see a body lying on the stage. Staring at the stage, without the camera, he could see nothing. But as soon as he looked through the view-finder, the body was back. Nothing ever showed up on the film.

The theatre witnessed other odd performances. Gilda took me down to the stage where I gawked at the ladders leading to the dizzyingly high catwalks. A few years ago a teenaged stagehand for the Civic Theatre was working up on the catwalk high above the stage when a fog drifted towards him. He began to back up and had almost run out of catwalk when a fellow stagehand climbed up the ladder. The fog disappeared as mysteriously as it had materialized.

Upstairs Gilda showed me the chilly projection room where she and others have heard keys jingling in some phantom's pocket. Some people have suggested that one of the ghosts is a former owner who spent all of his time there. Mysterious footsteps have been heard climbing the stairs to the projection booth area.

"Now up here," Gilda said, as she unlocked the door to the third floor, "We're entering into another world."

We climbed the creaking stairs in a stairwell with original plaster walls and gas fixture. Upstairs the painted Masonic Ballroom still retain its original hardware cast with Masonic emblems. In the ritual room, frescoed Knights Templar stand in painted niches, a rare survival, found under many layers of wallpaper.

In spite of the grisly events of 1918, the Majestic has a vibrant atmosphere with nothing depressing or terrifying about it. A team of volunteers works hard to bring live theatre, second-run movies, and special Halloween events—like the "haunted hotel," just next door....

That's where things got chilling for me. The hotel adjoins the theatre and is reached through a connecting hall. So much turbulent energy swirled up the corridor into my face that I had to take a step backward. The first hotel rooms we saw stood empty except for some props and scenery, some spattered with "blood" and scary slogans from the haunted house tours.

Looking up the stairs at the open stairwell, I got the impression of someone dodging in and out of rooms, just a step ahead of us. Gilda gestured at the stairway to the second floor.

"That's where I had an experience," Gilda told me. "That's where I saw the Grim Reaper."

She had been sent to get a prop from a Civic Theatre storeroom in the abandoned hotel. As she was halfway up the steps to the second floor, someone called to her. She turned, and midway down the steps, she saw this "grim reaper thing in a big hood" gliding along the hall by the second-floor railing. It drew up alongside her and looked at her.

"If I could have seen a face—if there *had* been a face—our eyes would have locked. I couldn't take my eyes off of it. I kept walking down the stairs and it walked alongside me. I told the Civic Theatre girl they'd have to fetch things themselves."

Other apparitions at the Majestic have been more benign:

A man wearing a dark suit and a top hat has been seen walking down the main aisle, floating further and further up from the floor as he approaches the stage. Gilda explained this odd apparition, "It didn't make sense until the renovation a few years ago. When the plaster was taken off the walls, you could see the original floor was level from the lobby to the stage. Apparently he was walking where the floor was in his time."

Three men who spent a night on the stage told a chilling story. "They searched the theater from top to bottom to make sure they were the only ones there and then they went to sleep. Two of the men were sleeping on the left side of the stage and the other on the right. The two on the left woke up several times during the night by someone asking for 'Andrew.' None of the three men had that name."

Two actresses with the Civic Theatre just couldn't get their lines right. They stayed late for additional rehearsal. When they finally mastered the parts, they heard clapping from the balcony. Although the lights were down in the theatre, they could see enough to tell that no one was sitting in the balcony.

A ghostly little girl has been heard laughing and seen darting among dressing rooms. Usually people just glimpse her in their mirrors, but a Civic Theatre actress named Jill saw her clearly "face-to-face. In 3-D! She looked like she was asking for help. I practically cried—she looked so helpless. I didn't know what to do."

When the Cash Explosion lottery show filmed at the Majestic, the cast did a run-through before opening the theatre doors to the audience. The engineer asked for quiet, then began a sound check. As he did so, a young girl was heard singing. The engineer knew that a member of the staff had his little girl with him and assumed she was fooling around as children will.

"Cut it out!" he said impatiently. The singing got louder.

"Enough is enough!" he said. The voice mimicked him.

"OK," he said, slamming out the door, "where is she?"

He found the suspect little girl out back with her dad. She had no microphone, no equipment with which she could have transmitted her voice into the theatre.

"It isn't me!" she protested. But at the next sound check, the little girl's voice came back, cruelly imitating what he said until he was a nervous wreck.

Gilda finds the balcony to be a particularly active area of the Majestic. She and a friend were watching *The Ghost and the Darkness* in the balcony when her friend jumped.

"What's wrong?" Gilda whispered.

"My hair just raised up," the friend whispered back. She wasn't speaking figuratively. Gilda could see the woman's hair hanging in mid air above her shoulder, as if someone had picked it up and was examining it.

Gilda reported that my visit seems to have stirred things up. On July 15th, Gilda got a phone call from an irate woman. Someone had frightened her elderly father by calling his unlisted number at 12:52 a.m. and 7:15 a.m. that morning and the theatre's number had shown up on his caller-id.

"I want to know who works for you who would be calling my dad!" she demanded.

Gilda thought fast. She knew that members of the Civic Theatre had been working in the theatre that night. She gave the woman the names of the members, but none of them sounded familiar.

"I'll call security," she told the woman. "they monitor the time the place was locked up. They can tell us if anyone came in during the night."

Security told her that the theatre had been locked up at 12:13 a.m. and nobody else came into the building until 9:56 a.m. Gilda called the lady back with this unsettling news and offered to monitor the phones very closely in the future. "I didn't want to tell her we have a ghost...."

So who watches from the Majestic's balcony? Who dashes along the dressing-room corridors? And who, on or off this earth, made those phone calls? The playful little girl? The busy former theatre owner? The faceless Grim Reaper? Or some of the Reaper's soldier-victims?

Take your pick. They're all on the program—at the Majestic Theatre.

"YOU CAN CALL ME GEORGE"
The ghost at the Masonic Temple

How fares it with the happy dead?
-Alfred Lord Tennyson-

The Dayton Masonic Temple stands on a hill overlooking Interstate 75, commanding and magnificent. It is dramatically lit at night and you can't miss it, day or night. Built between 1926-1928, it is on the National Registry of Historic Places and has recently undergone an ambitious course of restoration.

I went in the discreet back door and was greeted by Neil Smalley, 1995-96 Masonic Grand Master for Ohio, and his wife, Willa Jean, who had originally invited me to visit. They were a handsome couple, bronzed and beautifully dressed, who looked like they had just stepped off a yacht. They introduced me to Mr. Smith, the Scottish Rite Secretary. He wore thick, dark-rimmed glasses, and a misty smile, as if his thoughts were far away. He was, as I was to soon find out, a walking encyclopedia of facts and figures about the building, its history, and membership.

Mr. Smalley and Mr. Smith took me up to a mezzanine above the large ballroom. Looking down into the shadowy room below, I imagined the banquets—everyone stiffly posed for the wide-angle camera, the event name and date grease-penciled at the bottom of the exposure; the dances under a mirrored crystal ball; the clatter of china, silver, and crystal. I caught a glimpse of something lighter in a dark area of tables under the mezzanine. Something that had been looking up at me was just dissolving.

I walked into the darkness at the far end of the mezzanine. I put my fingertips on a large metal door and closed my eyes, trying to make my mind a blank, thinking, "I'm not alone."

A flash of light made me open my eyes. A door leading off the mezzanine had been flung open; a man was silhouetted in the entrance, the light beyond him partly obscured by his body. I realized that the door was still shut, that the man was a ghost.

He was beaming so broadly, I never thought to be afraid. He was an older gentleman, neither short nor tall, and a bit on the stout side. He was bald, with a fringe of silver hair, a distinctive, egg-shaped head, and a very dapper mustache. He had a delightfully good-humored face and I knew instantly he was what an earlier generation would have called a "card." The life of the party, the practical jokester, the hail-fellow-well-met. He made a little bow and a sweep of the hand as if to say, "Come on in. I'll be your guide for today's tour."

Bemused by his vivid presence, I went on into a cafeteria area, watching and listening. I heard voices and footsteps coming up a stairway. Then I realized they were real people—cooks in the kitchen below—and decided against going into that area. I didn't want to make anyone nervous. I was nervous enough.

The men ushered me into the robing area, filled with cupboards and green-painted lockers like sarcophagi standing on end. Masonic ritual includes theatrical performances and there were robes of velvet sewn with glass jewels, soldier's garb studded with metal discs, wigs, crowns, capes, and staffs. Mr. Smalley showed me a huge walnut Eastlake pier mirror that he loved. I wondered if it ever reflected the past. In another room, wigs on head-shaped stands eerily resembled decapitated heads. Something darted behind a costume rack.

A strong breeze swept down at me from a stair that I was told led to the stage. I walked into one of the make-up rooms. Their upright barber chairs looking expectant and somehow alert, ready for a shave or trim at a moment's notice. I examined a cracked window in the back of the make-up room. The breeze wasn't coming from there, it came from the stairs. I stepped back and looked up. At the top of the stairs stood the same old gentlemen, beaming down at me. I smiled back.

"You can call me George," he said. Ghosts rarely talk to me; usually I just get an impression of what they want. But this time I got real words and I was both surprised and pleased.

The two men led me through a maze of corridors, stairways, and rooms for instruction, study, meditation. Sometimes we took an elevator to one floor; sometimes we took stairs. I was completely confused about just where I was in the building. But George was always there, radiating friendliness.

The lounge was another matter altogether. I shuddered, just looking at the shadowed darkness beyond the heavy portieres. It was clear that I had crossed a boundary when I passed through the curtained arch. My stomach hurt. It was *not* friendly. I felt like I had accidentally crashed a men's club in London where a couple of retired colonels looked at me over the top of their newspapers and snorted with irritation, "You don't belong here!" "What's *she* doing here?"

The room looked as though it hadn't changed since the building was built in 1927. Faded olives, browns, and burgundies. Brocades, velvets. Beamed ceilings; fringed lamps; old, dark wood. The cushions of the chairs were crumpled, as if the owners had just thrown down their newspapers and gone to complain about this intruder in the reading room.

In a corner, at the far end of the room, a little out of place in all the neo-Flemish-Spanish-Jacobean-Tudor splendor, stood a television set. Two tubby chairs huddled in front of the TV and in one of them, a ghostly man sagged to one side. I could only see the back of his head and part of one shoulder, but something about the way he lay disturbed me. I wanted to tiptoe over to see if he was breathing. I edged out of the lounge.

Up the hall, in the library, I was surprised to find it blindingly lit by the late afternoon sun. Time had seemed to stand still as I was exploring the Temple. I examined some plaques on the wall listing various members and found a familiar name: Judge Elam Fisher, who haunted Fisher Hall at Miami University (See "The Old School Spirits" chapter in *Haunted Ohio*). I also found several Georges but my friendly apparition didn't give a last name.

In a room labeled 2M-B, I found a severe-looking man in a dark, double-breasted suit sitting at the desk. He had a scholarly-looking goatee and wore pince-nez glasses. He was tall, thin and had dark hair and he seemed to be from the 1920s or 30s. He seemed to be an examiner of some sort, and I was certain that, no matter what the subject, I would have flunked!

In what was called the "Commandary" I once again felt that punched in the stomach feeling and became short of breath. This was an imposing room with an upper gallery, colorful wall paintings, and a magnificent pipe organ. Mr. Smith told me that the Temple boasts seven full-size pipe organs. The figure of a man was near the organ. Somehow my "friend" was not with me here and I felt fear.

We explored the Billiard Room and another robing room, but I felt nothing. I was getting drained. At one point, Mr. Smalley said, "We've shown you lots of large rooms, now we'll show you a small one." He switched the light on in a tiny cell of a room, with some chairs against one wall and a small tripod table. I immediately got the impression of a seance being held, something I was almost certain was impossible.

Mr. Smalley switched on the lights in the game room. A few boxes of playing cards were scattered on the tables. I had been walking and sensing for nearly two hours and I was exhausted. I sat down in a chair and leaned my chin on my hand. While I was zoning out at the card table, "George" came up behind me, cupped his hand under my elbow and scooped me out of my chair. "Come on, Girly," he said jovially.

I smiled and shook my head as I obediently got up and moved on.

I asked to use the lady's room and was guided to a sad little lounge filled with faded chintz furniture. I caught a fleeting glimpse of a big-bosomed lady dressed in the fashions of the 1930s or 40s, rather like Margaret Dumont of the Marx Brothers' comedies. I didn't linger any longer than I needed to.

Before I went up to Mr. Smalley's office, I was shown into a chilly room called the Board of Directors' Room. George irreverently propped his feet on the desk. Along one end of the sparsely furnished Parquet Room, was a set of photos held in swinging poster display racks, one photo of each "class" per year. Idly I started looking through them, starting with, I believe, 1954.

"1962," said George. I flipped to 1962, ran my finger down the rows of stiffly posed men—and there was George, or someone who looked very much like George, sitting at the end of a row. Under his mustache, his smile was artificial and didn't convey his warmth at all. "Your picture doesn't do you justice," I said. I looked closely at every man in the 1962 shot and at several other photos, but nobody else came close to resembling "George" with his distinctive egg-shaped head.

Pondering this, and nursing a terrible headache, I headed back to Mr. Smalley's office. A little group of people began to assemble in the comfortable, well-lit office. One lady told me some stories of apparitions and death omens from the hills of West Virginia. One gentleman with a soft, thoughtful voice, wondered if I was a psychic and asked many questions about what it was like to see ghosts.

When we were all there, I began. I was quite nervous. My previous three visits to various allegedly haunted homes had turned up zero ghosts and I had begun to wonder if my abilities had deserted me. I sat directly opposite Secretary Smith.

I started by outlining a little of my background, how I do my work, and some different types of hauntings.

Feeling ridiculous I said, "This is going to sound very silly, but you don't hold seances, do you?" I was pretty certain the Masons did no such thing, but the tiny room with its tripod table and few chairs gave the overwhelming impression of questions asked and answered.

"That's an examination room," Mr. Smalley explained. "Candidates have to pass an oral exam before they can go on to the next degree."

"Oh!" I said, suddenly enlightened—that was the impression of the seance: questions and answers.

I ran through my pages of notes; Mr. Smith smiled slightly and bobbed his head whenever I said something that seemed to please him. Apparently I was hitting most of the spots correctly. The leaning man in the chair in the lounge was old Mr. Fredericks*, who had dozed in that spot by the hour, and who had been carried from that chair to the hospital, stricken with his fatal stroke. All of the women agreed that they hated to go into the lounge: that they always felt that they were being watched there.

In addition, I was told that people visiting the Temple after hours hear the sound of ladies' high-heel shoes clicking briskly along on the mezzanine, even though no one is there. The water fountain by the elevator comes on as if someone is taking a drink, and then stops. Doors open and close by themselves. The elevators run and open as if a living person is riding them, but no one ever gets off. Billiard players have reported that someone seems to sit and watch the games. And, said Mr. Smalley, many of the security people, who are there 24 hours a day, have reported seeing a ghostly man.

After I had completely finished, another man came into the room. In his double-breasted suit and hand-painted tie, he looked like the hard-boiled guy in a 1940s detective thriller; a non-nonsense kind of man. Even though I felt I'd been pretty successful at picking out the haunt spots within the building, I wasn't feeling completely secure and his piercing blue eyes rattled me. He admitted to a belief in the supernatural and told us fascinating stories of his experiences in the Temple, but he told them strictly off the record. He did not want to be identified, so I'll call him Mr. Marlowe.*

He seemed quite interested in my friend George.

"She's got a photo of him," one of the ladies chimed in.

"Yes, in one of the class pictures," I said.

"Well, I'm not going to describe him," said Mr. Marlowe firmly. "Let's go see this photo." He stood up.

We all trooped off down the hall. I clacked through the metal frames to the 1962 picture.

"There," I said, and backed away, while the others crowded around the photo.

Mr. Marlowe leaned forward, then turned around, half-smiling, shaking his head in a baffled sort of way. I thought he looked a little pale.

"That's him," he said. "That's the guy I see all the time. He's not dressed like that, but that's him." Then, with an anxiety to be exact that I admired, he added, "At least, that's what the guy I see looks like."

Nobody knew who the man in the 1962 photo was. Mr. Smith said he would check the class roster for the name at the first opportunity. Oddly, when he did check, he was unable to locate the class roster for 1962. George's identity will remain a mystery a while longer.

Rarely have I felt so comfortable with a spirit. He obviously never met a person he didn't like and it showed in his warm smile and courtly manners. He followed me almost everywhere in the Temple, although not into the ladies' lounge. He was, after all, a perfect gentleman. Headache and all, I was still smiling at his cheerful demeanor as I drove away. George was, and apparently still is, a credit to his colleagues.

I don't know for certain why George stays. I don't think he's one of those spirits who doesn't know he's dead and is caught between worlds. I think he has simply chosen to stay in a place he loved in life.

There are fewer and fewer Masons these days; its members are aging and young men rarely come to replace them. Some- day the Temple may be only a beautiful monument to a lost tribe. As each member joins George in that realm beyond life, perhaps they will carry on, reading their newspapers in the lounge, playing billiards or cards, robing in the dressing rooms—firm members of the Brotherhood, even unto death.

APPENDIX 1
FRIGHT BITES
More mini-tales of the macabre

This proved to be one of the most popular features of *Haunted Ohio III*, so here are some shorter, more anecdotal ghost tales. Some are little more than speculation or rumor, but some might deserve more investigation. And remember that when I say "the ghost walks at midnight" I mean, "the ghost is *said* to walk at midnight."

Some firefighters have seen a shadowy figure or heard footsteps in the second-floor bunk room in the 110-year-old Franklin Street firehouse in Circleville. They could be the steps of Chief J.M. Baer, the only Circleville fire chief to die on duty, dropping dead of a heart attack after a run in 1926.[1]

There is a Crybaby Bridge on Butler County's Fudge Road where a woman supposedly hung herself after her child died. If you turn off your car and say, "mama, mama, mama," out the window, you'll hear a baby cry.

Ohio has multiple Death Angel statues. Legend says that touching the hand of a Holmes County angel in a cemetery near Saltillo on CR 310 off CR 68 brings bad luck the rest of the day. If you look into the angel's eyes, they will begin to glow and you will die within three days.[2]

The same story is told about "The Curse of St. Michael," a white marble statue of the Archangel Michael in the Catholic cemetery at St. Mary's which kills those who look into his eyes. One girl just glanced into his eyes and was paralyzed.

There is a less sinister angel statue in a cemetery in Cambridge that moves its arms as a miracle to prove that God exists.

The tombstones at Hartman Cemetery in Hancock County, nicknamed Hell, move. You can visit the cemetery, pick out a stone, and a week later, the stone will be in a different part of the grounds.

On Rt. 66 out of Spencerville in a very old cemetery is a small bench made of three cement slabs, where, if you sit there at the wrong moment, the souls of the dead will hold you until you die.

It sounded like such a good story.... The family grave is located in Ohio City's Woodlawn Cemetery, off to the right of 118 as you enter Ohio City. Farmer Phillip K. tired of his wife Jane, as husbands often do, and decided to do away with her. He threw a rope over a beam in the barn and called urgently for her to come out. Jane was sewing in the house when she heard his call. Tucking her scissors into her apron pocket, she went out to the barn.

Phillip took his wife by surprise as he threw a noose over her head and hauled on the other end of the rope. But as he pulled, she seized her scissors and stabbed her husband through the heart. When the neighbors found them, they were both dead; Jane's neck unnaturally elongated and Phillip sprawled in a pool of blood seething blackly with flies.

The monument that stands above their grave cost $9,500 in the early 1900s. The life-size statues that stand on the couple's grave show Phillip with his rope and Jane with her scissors. It is said that if you feel her hand, it will be warm. Touch his hand next, you will feel the same warmth. But if you touch her warm hand a second time, then touch his—his hand will be hot. Sometimes truth is less exciting than fiction. Certainly the couple stare dourly at each other over the sepulchre that separates them, but Jane carries sheep-shearing scissors; Phillip, stalks of wheat. To the casual observer—or a fanciful imagination—the stalks of wheat could resemble a rope and the shearers, murderous scissors. The dates are also a dead giveaway: Phillip died in 1908; Jane, in 1920.

A man known as the "Hermit on the Knob" shot himself at Beck's Knob at Shallenberger State Nature Preserve, Fairfield County. His ghost walks from the knob across the plain to Hunters Run Creek and disappears. At night his lantern can be seen atop the hill.

Nettle Lake was the home of a multi-tenacled beast called the Kraken which lurked in the lake-bottom ooze and dragged boaters to their doom.[3]

Miami University's Wilson Hall was once a tuberculosis hospital. It is still haunted by ghosts that scream and moan and overturn furniture.

Miami's Fisher Hall is now the Marcum Center, Employees report seeing elevators doors open and close by themselves.

Kathy* and her sister Karen* were asleep in their bedroom in Hamilton. Kathy awoke to find that a wheelchair left behind by a previous tenant was sitting in the doorway with a shadow like a person sitting in it. Normally the wheelchair was kept in the garage, but it wheeled itself into the room, stopped between her bed and Karen's, then went back into the other bedroom on the upstairs floor.

Near Bluffton was a house haunted by a soldier who was buried at the end of the lane in a spot known as Hesakiah's Grave. One weekend, the Petersons and some friends and co-workers went out to Hesakiah's Grave. They dared a guy to go inside the house from 11:45 to 12:15 a.m. He went inside and everyone could hear him whistling and singing to pass the time away. When it was 12:15 a.m. the guy came out of the house onto the porch and hollered. "There isn't anyone in this house!"

Just as he said that, someone dressed in a soldier's uniform stepped into the doorway behind him and started shooting a gun in the air. The next day Peterson and some of his buddies went back but couldn't find any shells. To this day, nobody knows who was in that soldier's uniform.[4]

In the middle of the Maumee River at Napoleon there are small islands covered with trees and tall grasses. On one of these islands, a soldier keeps watch all the time. If you land there and try to stay too long, he will chase you until you leave.

At Deshler, a drunk motorcyclist was dared by his drunken buddies to jump the creek without using the bridge—a span of about 20 feet. He missed the other side, went into the water and drowned. Now you can hear ghostly motorcycle noises at midnight beside the creek.

Rebecca was driving home one night from Eaton with two of her friends on US 127, when she came upon a car going very slow. As she passed it, she looked at the car and saw an old man driving while the car glowed inside. When she pulled in front of his car, he turned his headlights off and disappeared despite no turnoff roads on that stretch of 127.

Cry Baby Lane is the wooded, north-south stretch of Euler Road, which runs between Wingston Road and Potter Road, southwest of Bowling Green, where a mother hung her baby on a tree limb. When the wind blows, you can hear the baby crying and see it swinging back and forth.[5]

Darke County's Crybaby Bridge is haunted by the spirits of unwanted gypsy babies tossed off the bridge into the river.[6]

Holcomb Road near Pemberville off State Route 199 is haunted by legends of a ghostly suicide and mysterious lights You may see two headlights in your rearview mirror, but if you look out the back window, the lights shoot off to one side and disappear.[7]

Another Cry Baby Bridge is located somewhere northwest of Bellefontaine. A father traveling home late one evening with his three children, crashed into the bridge. The stillness of the night is often shattered by the distant cry of the lonely baby, whose body was lost.[8]

The elusive Ghost Hill in Fredericktown was a high gravel bank containing Indian burials. The gravel was used in graveling local roads and the hill is now gone and no one knows exactly where it stood. Nancy A. Black who wrote an article on it for the *Knox County Citizen* says while she was photographing the approximate place where the hill stood, her film was ruined—twice.[9]

The corner of Darrow and Barrows Roads in Vermilion is haunted by the sound of a car which slammed into a utility pole. Residents often hear squealing tires, metal grinding and the plaintive cry of a small baby.

Late at night in Old Washington, you might hear the sound of horses hooves slowly approaching behind you. You might catch a quick glimpse of a black horse pulling a black buggy disappears when it is spotted.[10]

Athen's Simms Cemetery is haunted by victims of John Simms, the local hangman. Reports from Peach Ridge cemetery include the sighting of old man Simms appearing in a kind of mist, wearing a hooded robe like the specter of Death. He is reportedly kind and doesn't harm anyone. There are also reports of blood curdling screams heard at night on Peach Ridge. The screaming comes first from one direction, then immediately from the opposite.[11]

The John Bryan State Park camping area is haunted at dusk by a man who walks out the west gate, disappearing just before he reaches Meredith Rd. The ghost wears denim overalls, a blue shirt, and a red kerchief around his throat. He also wears a dark felt hat and strides along, his left hand in his pocket, the right hand swinging free. Local people think the ghost might be one of the men who gave the land to Greene County for the park.

Schmidt's Sausage Haus' original German Village location in Columbus is said to be haunted by the founding father, J. Fred Schmidt.

An old house in New Westville or Progress was haunted by the ghost of a young bugler who came home from the War of 1812 and died there. His bugle was sometimes heard on still nights.[12]

"Restless John," whose family was killed in a fire that destroyed his house, is said to wander the site of his old house near Continental. In the abandoned house on his property, a disembodied man's voice has been heard and lights have been seen in the windows, explained as headlight glare until someone realized there was no glass in the windows. Everyone who has lived in the house has suffered some terrible misfortune.`[13]

A ghostly nun still rustles through the Glandorf house that had been her convent, trying doorknobs and scratching on doors. When graves on the property were moved, the farmer kept a rosary found with one of the bodies so perhaps the nun is looking for her beads.[13]

On the north side of Route 224 in Gilboa is a small cemetery where nearly all of the graves are of children who died in the cholera epidemic of 1952. It is said that the sound of children can be heard there late at night.[13]

"The Haunted Mound" was located in the northwest corner of Washington Township on a farm which once belonged to the Wegerly family. There were reports of ghostly lights and fog floating about or rocketing out of a mound even on clear nights. Sometime in the 19th century, an attempt was made to dig up the site, but so many strange things began to happen that the excavation was stopped. Someone also committed suicide near the spot and that led to the weird happenings.[14]

A house on S. Court St. in Circleville (now the Genealogical Library) is haunted by the spirits of runaway slaves, which local legend says were once sheltered in the basement of the home.[14]

Haines Cemetery in New Marshfield is reputed haunted by an insane Civil War officer driven by his war wounds to destroy his family homestead—and his family—with an ax.[15]

At Buckley House, 332 Front Street, Marietta, the ghost of William New Kim, an exchange student from China, desolately roams. He drank chloroform when his patroness objected to his "marriage" to a servant girl.[16]

Mid-Ohio Valley Players Theatre on Putnam Street in Marietta is haunted by a nattily-dressed man in a felt derby.[16]

When future President Warren G. Harding was married in 1891, among the wedding gifts was a wall clock that still hangs in the Harding Home and Museum in Marion, Ohio. The clock worked perfectly, even after Harding's death in 1923. But on August 2, 1973, at 7:30 p.m., the clock inexplicably stopped. Mrs. Harold Augestein, the museum's curator, noted that the time was the exact hour of Harding's death, precisely 50 years before. Efforts were made during the following week to get the clock started again. Finally on Thursday, one week later, the clock began to run—as mysteriously as it had stopped the previous Thursday.[17]

Supposedly the spirit of a prehistoric man with "humped back, thick hair, and a protruding forehead" lives in Orton Hall on the OSU campus in Columbus. Two Columbus psychics say that he cannot speak, but will bang on things, slam doors or make guttural noises to get attention. Orton Hall may also be haunted by Edward Orton, who makes noise and chills the air, trying to make students behave with decorum.[18]

There is a forest between Cadmus and Patriot called the "Shades of Death" where a jealous man hanged his wife because he couldn't trust her. The woman's ghost returns to the forest.[19]

Between Bidwell and Vinton is a place called Knox Hollow, where years ago twins sleepwalked into a nearby creek and began swimming, even though they normally could not swim. The father saw them swimming in deep water and yelled to them. They woke up , realized they were in deep water, and drowned. Occasionally they would come back in their "ghostly trunks" to take a dip.[19]

A ghostly cowbell haunted Reuben Tetirick's farm, two miles southwest of Winterset. It rang in the darndest places, like beneath the floor and under the daughter's bed. It was suggested that the farm's previous owner, the Widow Cramer, was keeping her promise to come back and haunt Tetirick, who had argued with her.[20]

In a jealous rage, a woodsman named Charlie in the area of Old Man's Cave and Conkle's Hollow State Parks chopped off the heads of his wife and the "other man" and threw them from the top of the triple-decker caves at Salt Pete into the ravine below. On quiet moonlit nights, you can still hear him chopping wood near the caves.

Ft. Hayes in Columbus is haunted by a ghost in World War II uniform, seen behind the Drill Hall who fell asleep on duty, was brought up on charges and died mysteriously in jail. He appears very anxious and very transparent, fading away when noticed.[21]

The Woods School [just north of Belmont] is haunted by a headless horseman who gallops up and commands, "Pull over there, stranger, and give me my saddlebags!" Four cattlemen sold their herd in Belmont in 1845. They rode toward the Black Horse Inn, their saddlebags bulging with money but never got there. Some 75 years ago, the remains of four saddlebags were found in the woods near the school.[22]

The ghost of a dead farmer chased a foxhunter into a pig pen at Matamoras Hill, Belmont County.[23]

In southwest Cleveland is a doctor's tiny office where footsteps are heard regularly in a vacant attic; vials and bottles fly across the room; and cold spots appear and vanish. In one case a woman brought her child to see the doctor not knowing the office was closed. She called the next day, complaining that "the old man in the waiting room," would not let her in the office, and ignored her shouts and poundings on the door, though he was only a few feet away. Office staff told her that the office door was locked and no one could have entered.[24]

The Dug Hill Bridge over the Auglaize River between Wapakoneta and Defiance was haunted by a man accidentally shot as he hunted deer by a deer lick. The ghost crossed the bridge at midnight and chased travelers.[25]

A ghost near Ft. Amanda was that of a woman "accidentally" shot by her husband who had eyes for another woman. One day he came home from a squirrel hunt and laid his gun on the bed and when he went to hang it up, it fired, killing his wife. He married his other woman, but for a long time the first wife's spirit hovered about the home at night.[25]

The spirit of an Indian haunts an area on Cty Rd 175 near Ashland/Wayne Co Line. He walks along the creek bed looking for ash and hickory wood for tomahawk handles.[26]

There are at least two ghosts at Lima Correctional Institute. One is a "presence" that tucks in prisoners. The other is a Lima State Hospital matron who brings food to the inmates. She has enough reality that when trays are delivered, inmates say that they've already been fed. Employees see the woman and can even give her employee number—the number of a matron who worked at the hospital years ago.[27]

The Lockington Dam area, a popular parking spot, is reputedly haunted by werewolves who scratch the sides of cars, howl, and leave trails of blood along the bridge.

At Wolfe Mausoleum, in Centerville Cemetery there is a legend that two pet wolves were buried alive with their owner and you can still hear them howling.

Headless Hattie, a decapitated murder victim haunts several roads around Prospect: Owens or Gooding. Someone broke into her house and robbed her, beat her, and cut her head off. From then on, some people would see her body wandering around looking for her head.

Somewhere in the rolling farmland between Greenville, Ansonia and Versailles is a steel-framed bridge surrounded by thick woods. Back in the days when this was the Indians' land, the woods swarmed with werewolves who picked off the weak, the young and the old, leaving behind a bloody trail into the woods. When the pioneers moved in, they built a covered bridge so the werewolves couldn't get at travellers. The creatures have practically died out, but a full moon brings a werewolf's blood to the boil. And on full-moon nights, you can hear the call of the werewolf.[28]

At Ft. Recovery, in Mercer County, a 10-ft., red-eyed creature, part-wolf, part-woman, was spotted in the woods and on the bridge.

Game warden Joe Steele caught a three-foot alligator at Huffman Dam in Dayton.[29]

Whenever anyone crosses the bridge at Denmark, an eerie light—supposedly a lantern held by the hand of an unseen entity—hovers over the water of the St. Joseph River to escort the party across the bridge. Richard Cooley and Don Allison investigated the haunting in 1982 and found that the "lantern" was the reflection of the moonlight on the St. Joseph River.[30]

A farmer in Hocking Township took in a young boy to raise, promising him $300 and a horse when he reached age 21. Shortly after the Civil War began he disappeared and the farmer claimed he had enlisted in the Union Army. The farmer sold the farm. The new owner noticed a weird light floating about the farm at night, disappearing at a stone pile west of the barn where a party of farmers found a man's skeleton.[31]

In March of 1897, the unidentified body of a middle-aged, well-dresssed man, with his throat slashed from ear to ear was found near a railroad crossing, having washed out from beneath a culvert beneath the Zanesville and Maysville Road. His ghost, a gaping wound in his throat was seen pacing the highway in the Delmont vicinity.[31]

Coney Island's Moonlite Gardens are haunted by an old woman and a young man who look out of the music pavilion's first-floor windows; by mysterious fogs that settle over the park on a clear night; and by ghostly Indians whose war-chants can be heard in the nearby picnic groves.[32]

Van Campen Hall at Kent State University was haunted in the early 1970s by "Nathan Richards" who came through on the ouija board claiming to have been born in the 1830s and hanged for murder in Dayton. Dayton records showed that Richards actually existed and was indeed hanged for murder in the 1850s. The spirit created poltergeist-like activity both at Korb Hall, where the original ouija session took place and at Van Campen, where the two students moved the next fall.[33]

The Worthington Inn is haunted by a previous owner whose habit in life was to walk through the kitchen and the dining room, dusting the chairs and tables, smoking his trademark cigar, then check the cash register. Staff has heard him walking through the kitchen and dining room, smelled his cigar, and heard the ringing of an old-time cash register.

WNRR Radio of Bellevue was haunted by footsteps on the stairs leading to their offices. After the the stairway and hall were carpeted, the footsteps disappeared. It is believed that the footsteps belong to a vagrant who died in the building. Employees also catch a fleeting glimpse of a figure scurrying past the control room window.[34]

The 1832 cottage where Alice Cary saw the apparition of her little sister Lucy (see *Haunted Ohio*) now stands on the grounds of the Clovernook Center for Opportunities. About 1980, two young girls moved from Detroit into a house across the street from Clovernook. Soon after the move, one of them asked their mother, "Who is that little girl in the red dress I keep seeing in the window of Cary Cottage?"[35]

A spook light appears at Weidler's Passing track M.P. 1054 near Arcadia. Trains often would be stopped by a lantern swinging back and forth across the tracks. When the trainmen got off their train to investigate, the ghosts of trainmen killed in an accident would disappear into the nearby woods. Other times, the light would keep just so far ahead of the train, which never could catch up; and by the time the train reached Weidlers, the light would shoot off into the sky.

It was a dark and stormy night. In November, 1968, Ruth and her mother, along with Ruth's baby daughter, were on the Ohio Turnpike, traveling from Strongsville to Youngstown. "Somewhere before we passed the Lordstown GM Plant, we both drew in a sharp breath at the same time. Mom instinctively took her foot off the gas pedal. Crossing the road in front of us, north to south, a black apparition on a black night, was a stagecoach pulled by four horses. The driver was half-standing and it was going like the wind!"

County Road 19, which crosses Hog Creek/the Ottawa River just south of Route 114 between Kalida and Cloverdale, is said to be haunted by a ghostly young beauty killed on her prom night. She stands in the middle of the bridge, wearing a long formal gown and corsage, and has been known to send motorists spinning into a ditch to avoid hitting her.[36]

At Bonnyconnellan Castle in Sidney the owner has seen a man in a blue uniform staring at the wedding dress displayed on the stair landing.

There was a well in Lee Township, about five miles from Sardis in Monroe County where a woman threw her out-of-wedlock child to drown. It was said that you could hear the child cry if you walked by the well after dark.

Near the Old National Trail Riding Center in Englewood is a springhouse, a sinister, twisted Hanging Tree, and the remains of Pattys House. Some stories say that the Pattys sisters were hung from the Hanging Tree by a relative and that they scream and chill the air around the site.

APPENDIX 2
HAUNTED PLACES
Sites open to the public

AUGLAIZE CO.
   Ft. Amanda, 22783 St Rt 198, Cridersville, OH
BROWN CO.
   Baird House, 201 N 2nd St., Ripley, OH 45167 (937) 392-4918
BUTLER CO.
   Miami University, Oxford, OH 45403. Marcum Hall and Wilson Hall still stand.
CLERMONT CO.
   Smyrna Cemetery, Smyrna Road, 1/2 mile e. of Felicity.
COLUMBIANA CO.
   Beaver Creek State Park, East Liverpool, OH (216) 385-3091
CUYAHOGA CO.
   Kohler Hall, Baldwin-Wallace College, Berea, OH
FRANKLIN CO.
   Camp Chase Confederate Cemetery, Contact Hilltop Historical Society, 2456 W. Broad St., Columbus, OH 43204 (614) 276-0060
      Schmidt's Sausage Haus, 240 E Kossuth St, Columbus, OH
      Worthington Inn, 649 High St, Worthington, OH 43085
GREENE CO.
   Olde Trail Tavern, 228 Xenia Avenue, Yellow Springs, OH 45387

HAMILTON CO.
>	*Cary Cottage,* Clovernook Center for Opportunities, 7000 Hamilton Ave, Cincinnati, 45231 (513) 522-3860

LAKE CO.
>	*Rider's 1812 Inn,* 792 Mentor Ave., Painesville, OH 44007 (216) 354-8200

LICKING CO.
>	*The Buxton Inn,* 313 E. Broadway, Granville, OH 43023 (614) 587-0001

MEDINA CO.
>	*Spitzer House Bed & Breakfast,* 504 West Liberty St., Medina, OH 44256 (330) 725-7289

MONTGOMERY CO.
>	*Dayton Masonic Temple,* 525 W. Riverview Ave, (937) 224-9795. Tours by appointment ONLY.
>	*Pattys House,* Old National Trail Riding Center, 930 Pattys Rd., Englewood, OH 45377. Park at the stable parking lot, then turn left out of the parking lot and walk about 100 yards up the road until you see a dirt road blocked by some posts. Walk up that road to the hanging tree and house site.
>	*Sinclair Community College,* 444 W. Third St., Dayton, OH 45402
>	*United States Air Force Museum,* Springfield Street, Gate 28-B, Wright-Patterson Air Force Base, Dayton, OH
>	*University of Dayton,* 300 College Park Ave, Dayton, OH, 45409
>	*Woodland Cemetery,* 118 Woodland Ave., Dayton, OH 45409 (513) 222-1431

ROSS CO.
>	*The Majestic Theatre,* 45 East 2nd St., Chillicothe, OH 45601-2543, (614) 772-2041

SHELBY
>	*Bonnyconnellan Castle,* 105 Walnut Ave., Sidney, OH, (937) 497-9200 FEE FOR TOURS

VAN WERT CO.
>	*Woodlawn Cemetery,* to the right of Rt. 118 as you enter Ohio City, eight miles south of Van Wert.

WOOD CO.
>	*Bowling Green State University,* Theatre Department, BGSU, Bowling Green, OH 45403 (419) 372-2222

MORE GHOSTLY TALES

(Also see the bibliographies in *Haunted Ohio, Haunted Ohio II, Haunted Ohio III* and *Spooky Ohio*.)

Once again, let me plug my *Invisible Ink®* catalog, listing over 500 ghostly titles from around the world. These are mostly non-fiction books like *Haunted Louisiana, Haunted Houses of California, Ghostly Tales of Tasmania.* For your free copy call 1-800-31-GHOST.

All of the items in this bibliography can (as of this writing) be ordered through *Invisible Ink®*.

Cartmell, Connie, *Ghosts of Marietta*, 1996
> A delightful look at the river-front spirits of this picturesque town including "George," a sorority spirit, the sad Chinese exchange student at Buckley House, and the murdered man at The Levee House Cafe.

Crawford, Richard, *Uneasy Spirits: 13 Ghost Stories from Clermont County, Ohio,* 1997
> Rick Crawford knows where all the bodies are buried in Clermont County and where their ghosts haunt and he doesn't hesitate to dish the [grave] dirt.

Crites, Susan, *Ghosts Along the Potomac*, 1996
> Susan has a gift for getting people who might be your next-door neighbors to tell their extraordinary stories. These West Virginia stories are beautifully written, first-hand, recent sightings and they are most unsettling.

Hauck, Dennis William, *Haunted Places: The National Directory, Ghostly abodes, sacred sites, UFO landings, and other supernatural locations,* 1996
> This is the new and updated version. Most of the Ohio stories come from my books and they are not always accurately reported. Still, the best general directory to haunt-spots mortal money can buy.

Henson, Michael Paul, *More Kentucky Ghost Stories,* 1996
> A wonderful collection of traditional and contemporary tales from the hills. Henson has a real feel for ghostly re-enactments and time-warps. You'll also enjoy his *Tragedy at Devil's Hollow and Other Kentucky Ghost Stories,* 1984

Mead, Robin, *Haunted Hotels: A Guide to American and Canadian Inns and Their Ghosts,* 1995
> More than 100 motel hells recommended by a travel writer who found them clean, comfortable, a good value—and reputed to be haunted. This is the ultimate travel guide. Gives addresses and phones so you can book a haunted holiday.

Montell, William Lynwood, *Ghosts Along the Cumberland, Deathlore in the Kentucky Foothills,* 1975
> To me, a very frightening book. Crisis apparitions, death omens, funeral practices, and deathlore from the hills.

Montell, William Lynwood, *Kentucky Ghosts,* 1994
> More "haint" tales from folklorist Montell.

Norman, Michael & Beth Scott, *Haunted America, Vol. 1,* 1994
> At least one story from all fifty states collected and told by the masterful duo who created *Haunted Heartland,* 1988.
> If you like haunted historic sites, you'll enjoy Scott and Norman's *Historic Haunted America* (Haunted America, Vol. 2), 1995
> All-new eyewitness accounts of historic hauntings that may still be waiting for a sensitive observer.

Okonowicz, Ed, *Possessed Possessions, Haunted Antiques, Furniture and Collectibles,* 1996
> Twenty-one strange stories of haunted objects including several Ohio tales. Real this and you'll never buy antiques again. A fascinating and unique book.

REFERENCES

Chapter One - Houses of Horror

[1] Anne Wolf, "Our Ghost Story," *FATE* (Jan. 1951) 29-35

[2] Amy D. Potter, *Ghostlore of Wood County, Ohio, Haunts and Hauntings*, unpublished paper for Pop Culture 325, (April 30 1987) 6-8

Chapter Two - Haunted Highways

[1] Earl Leon Heck, *Tales and Sketches of the Great Miami Valley*, (Englewood, OH: n.p.) 26 Mar. 1962

[2] L. Gregory Thurston, "Bride in white seen roaming along Trebein Road after dark," *Fairborn Daily Herald*, 28 Oct. 1996

[3] Ed Butts, "Deep Mysteries, The Great Lakes have their share of ghosts, goblins, and monsters, "The Strange Story of the Success, *Lakeland Boating* (Oct. 1993) 39-42

[4] Herb Barlow, "Saved from Disaster By a Phantom Auto," *FATE* (June 1994) 53-4

Chapter Three - You Always Haunt the One You Love

[1] Charles Wallace Harrison, "The Mystery of Pearce House," *[Cadiz]News-Herald*, 10 June 1982 B-4, no. 30; 17 June 1982 B-4, no. 31; 24 June 1982 C-4, no. 32; 1 Jul. 1982 B-4, no. 33

Chapter Four - The Can-Do Spirit

[1] Rev. Asa Mahan, First President of Cleveland University, *Modern Mysteries Explained and Exposed*, (Boston: John P. Jewett and Company, 1855) 147-48

[2] Barbara Martin, "The Ghostly Dishwasher", *FATE* (July 1951) 14

Chapter Five - Ghosts That Would Crack a Mirror

[1] *UD Flyer News*, 30 Oct. 1986

Chapter Six - Lions and Tigers and Scares, Oh My!

[1] "Portage County Village Baffled by Dead Baboon," *Columbus Dispatch*, 17 Nov. 1996 7A

[2] "Deputies Track Fuzzy Observer," *Columbus Dispatch*, 11 Oct. 1973 1B

[3] Jim Babcock and Terrence L. Johnson, "Neither hide nor hair seen of 2 animals," *Dayton Daily News,* 29 May 1994

[4] *The [Cleveland] News Herald*, 28 Nov. 1994 and *Dayton Daily News*, 28 Nov. 1994

[5] *The Gate*, (Oct. 1992) 15

[6] Charles Warnick, "Dog-Gone Spooky! Carthage Plant Guards Keep on Seeing Eerie Figure and Canine in Fadeaway Act," *Cincinnati Enquirer*, 5 Aug. 1948 8

[7] *The Gate* (July 1997) 15

[8] Thomas J. Sheeran, "Rumors still floating around about whether Lake Erie Monster exists," *Dover-New Philadelphia Times-Reporter*, 31 Oct. 1993 A-2

[9] "Monster 'serpent' appears along Lake Erie shoreline" *Dayton Daily News*, 18 July 1993

[10] *Cleveland Plain Dealer*, 16 June 1985 25-A, 32-A

[11] Kevin Harter, "Big fish stories catch Ohio's fancy, 'Bessie' sightings stump scientists", *Dayton Daily News*, 7 Oct. 1990

[12] "Monster 'serpent' appears along Lake Erie shoreline," *Dayton Daily News,* 18 July 1993

Chapter Seven - Possessed Possessions

[1] Harry Nix, "The case of the mission macaroni," *FATE* (Feb. 1971) 92-95

[2] "Could mysterious horse have been an angel," Frances E. McCoy, Pikes Past Column, Jim Henry, *The News Watchman*, 24 Feb. 1994 9

Chapter Eight - They're Baaack!

[1] Editors, *Blue & Gray Magazine*, "13 Haunted Places of the Civil War, II the Sequel," *Blue & Gray Magazine*, "The Kind Ladies of Old Camp Chase," (Oct. 1991) 26-30

[2] Cindy Swavel, "Residents turn out to track down famed Lincoln ghost train," *Bucyrus Telegraph Forum*, 2 May 1995 also John Switzer, "Time may be right for Ghost Train," *Columbus Dispatch*, 6 April 1995

[3] Tara Gujadhur, "A NEW SPIRIT? "The hallowed halls of wisdom may not be hollow," *The Clarion*, 7 June 1994

[4] Joy Mullholand, "I Heard It Through the Grapevine," *[Bowling Green], Miscellany Magazi*ne, (Autumn 1992) 12

[5] *Athens News Messenger*, (Vol. 17 issue 86) 28 Oct. 1993

Chapter Nine - A Ghostly Miscellany

[1] Rod Senter, *Phantasm* (May 1994) 4-7

Chapter Ten - Doom at the Inn

1 Kim Bishop, "Portrait of a Haunting," *Etc.* Oct. 1994 7

Chapter Eleven - A Seance of Spooks

[1] Marion Snyder, "Memory Lane," *The Lebanon Star* 14 Jan 1985

Chapter Thirteen - Murder Most Phantom

[1] Bronsart Gilberg, *History of Mercer County*, (*Mercer County Historical Society*, 1980) 72

[2] *Cincinnati Enquirer*, 31 Oct. 1996 C-1, C-3

[3] David J. Gerrick, "Stoney Creek Cemetery," *Ohio's Ghostly Greats*, (Lorain: Dayton Press, 1982) 73-74

[4] Jim McGuire, "Stalking the shrieking ghost of White Lady Point," *Miami Valley Sunday News* 27 Oct. 1991 15

Chapter Fourteen - Working-Class Stiffs

[1] The Writers' Program of the Works Projects Administration in the State of Ohio, *Bryan and Williams County, Ohio,* 1941 80 Requoted in Howard L. Carvin, *The Bryan Times,* 26 Feb. 1954

Appendix 1 - Fright Bites

[1] Don Baird, "Ghost of Chief has firefighters listening closely," *The Columbus Dispatch*, n.d.

[2] Salina Chaney, "The Angel", *Rural Reflections*, Vol. One, (June 1986) 57

[3] *The Writers' Program of the Works Projects Administration in the State of Ohio, Bryan & Williams County*, 1941 78-9

[4] Jeanne Wiley, "Ghostly tales don't even faze area folklorist," *Lifestyles, Courier*, 24 Oct. 1989

[5] Amy D. Potter, *Ghostlore of Wood County, Ohio, Haunts and Hauntings*, unpublished paper for *Pop Culture* 325, 30 Apr. 1987 3-4

[6] *Darke County Daily Advocate*, 24 Oct. 1994 1

[7] Wendy M. King, "'Highway to Hell?' Holcomb Road is no traveler's paradise," *The [Bowling Green] Insider*, 15 Mar. 1991

[8] *Lima News* 31 Oct. 1983

[9] Nancy A. Black, "Chasing a town's ghost story," *Knox County Citizen*, 5 Sept. 1996

[10] *Daily Jeffersonian* 24 Oct. 1994 1

[11] Sandy Speidel, "Strange Tales of a Strange Town," *Athens Magazine,* (Fall 1973) 6-9 also *Athens Magazine*, (Spring/summer 1972) 35

[12] Irene Hardy, *An Ohio Schoolmistress, The Memoirs of Irene Hardy,* (Kent: Kent State Univ Press, 1980) 5

[13] Dave Westrick, "The Legend of Restless John and Other Ghost Stories," *Putnam County Sentinel*, 29 Oct. 1980 C also Dave Westrick, "Spirits of Past Abound In Franconia Cemetery," *Putnam County Sentinel*, 28 Oct. 1981 C

[14] Wallace Higgins, "Spectral speculations from Pickaway County," *Circleville Herald*, 27 Oct. 1993

[15] *Athens News* 30 Oct. 1980

[16] *Marietta Times,* 30-31 Oct 1993 1-D

[17] "Clock Marks Anniversary," *FATE* (Feb. 1975) 68

[18] Laura Crabbe, "Soul of prehistoric man flustered in Orton Hall," *OSU Lantern*, n.d. 1, 3

[19] Jim Sands, "Several Gallia County spots considered famous hauntings," *Galliopolis Sunday Times-Sentinel*, n.d. A8

[20] Dennis Bush, "How a ghostly cowbell made one man believe in the supernatural," *The Daily Jeffersonian*, 28 Oct. 1994 9

[21] John Switzer, "Fort Hayes ghosts await Halloween tours", *Columbus Dispatch,* 26 Oct. 1991

[22] "The Headless Horseman of Belmont," *FATE* (June 1956) 39

[23] *[Belmont County/Martins Ferry] Times-Leader* 25 Oct. 1992 1E, 5E

[24] *Cleveland Plain Dealer,* 15 April 1976 SU 6-11

[25] C.S. Lathrop, "History of Fort Amanda," *Auglaize County Historical Society News,* (Feb. 1979) #51 2-79

[26] *Ashland Times-Gazette* 31 Oct. 1994

[27] *Lima News* 31 Oct. 1990

[28] John Cummings, "A full-moon night brings them out," *[Greenville] Daily Advocate,* 27 Oct. 1994

[29] "Catches Alligator At Huffman Dam," *Dayton Daily News,* 7 July 1935 9 also *Dayton Journal* 7 July 1935. *The New York Times* 7 July 1935 2 erroneously reported that the catch was in Xenia.

[30] Richard L. Cooley, "Williams County Tales of Mystery: The Ghost Lantern at Denmark," *Northwest Historian,* (May 1992)

[31] Pauline Wessa, "Library compiling the chilling history of Fairfield ghosts," *Columbus Citizen Journal,* 7 Nov. 1980 4

[32] *Cincinnati Enquirer* 31 Jan. 1982

[33] *FATE* (Mar. 1971) 7

[34] "13 Local Haunts," *Lorain Morning Journal,* 30 Oct. 1994 A-8

[35] *Cincinnati Enquirer* 31 Jan. 1982

[36] Dave Westrick, "Young Beauty Continues to Haunt Rural Bridge," *Putnam County Sentinel,* 27 Oct. 1982 C

INDEX

GENERAL INDEX

NOTE: Roads are listed under "Roads" instead of individual street names

HOW TO ORDER YOUR OWN AUTOGRAPHED COPIES OF *SPOOKY OHIO* AND THE *HAUNTED OHIO* SERIES
(also T-Shirts, etc.)

Call **1-800-31-GHOST (1-800-314-4678)** with your VISA or MasterCard order or send this order form **Kestrel Publications, 1811 Stonewood Dr., Beavercreek, OH 45432 • (937) 426-5110**

☐ FREE CATALOG! **"INVISIBLE INK: Books on Ghosts and Hauntings"** - Over 500 books of ghost stories from around the world!

_____ copies of *SPOOKY OHIO* @ $8.95 each $_____

_____ copies of *HAUNTED OHIO* @ $10.95 each $_____

_____ copies of *HAUNTED OHIO II* @ $10.95 each $_____

_____ copies of *HAUNTED OHIO III* @ $10.95 each $_____

_____ copies of *HAUNTED OHIO IV* @ $10.95 each $_____

_____ *Spooky Ohio* **T-shirt** @ $12.00 each $_____
      Size ____M ____L ____XL ____XXL ____XXXL

_____ *Haunted Ohio* **T-shirt** @ $12.00 each $_____
      Size ____M ____L ____XL ____XXL ____XXXL

+ $2.50 Book Rate shipping, handling and tax for the first item, $1.00 postage for each additional item. Call (937) 426-5110 for speedier mail options. $_____

                          TOTAL $_____

NOTE: We usually ship the same or next day. Please allow three weeks before you panic. If a book *has* to be somewhere by a certain date, let us know so we can try to get it there on time.

MAIL TO (Please print clearly and include your phone number)

_____

_____

_____

FREE AUTOGRAPH!

If you would like your copies autographed, please print the name or names to be inscribed. _____

_____

PAYMENT MADE BY:

☐ Check ☐ MasterCard ☐ VISA
($15 min. order on credit cards)

Card No. _____

Signature _____

Expiration Date:

Mo_____ Yr_____